Berlitz

PARIS

POCKET GUIDE

STEAKS

100 m

100 m

DIAMANT
Restaurant

BROOKLAWN

JOE'S BURGERS
Restaurant

ARTS & CULTURE

Space disco
featuring th

Music

A TO Z INFO

SHOPPI

Shoppi
aroun
be fo

GATE BRIDGE

MAP

LIKE

SHARE

Sailing under the Golden Gate Bridge
today, it is interesting to consider that
engineers once thought it impossible to
span the Golden Gate Strait at this point,
because of the depth of the water (318ft/
97 meters, at its deepest point) and the
powerful tidal rush.

The city authorized studies for a bridge
in 1917, but it was 1933 before the first
shovel turned under the gaze of master
engineer Joseph B. Strauss (no relation
to the famous waltz composer), at a cost
years later the bridge opened, at a cost
of $35 million and the lives of 11
construction workers. Today the bridge

INSIGHT ⊙ GUIDES

SPAIN

≡

INTRODUCTION

EXPLOR

AILABLE

A

FLORIDA
This new edition of Insight Guide
Florida is a comprehensive, full-colour
land guide packed with inspiration
and information. It includes everything
from colonial turf that was and ...

FRANCE
This brand new edition Insight Guide
to France features outstanding
full-colour photography, which ties
together magnificent 150 brand new
photographs, alongside 250 brand new
explorations of all the places to go

LUCIA Pocket Guide

Walking Eye
mobile app

Discover the world's best destinations with the Insight Guides Walking Eye app, available to download for free in the App Store and Google Play.

The container app provides easy access to fantastic free content on events and activities taking place in your current location or chosen destination, with the possibility of booking, as well as the regularly-updated Insight Guides travel blog: Inspire Me. In addition, you can purchase curated, premium destination guides through the app, which feature local highlights, hotel, bar, restaurant and shopping listings, an A to Z of practical information and more. Or purchase and download Insight Guides eBooks straight to your device.

TOP 10 ATTRACTIONS

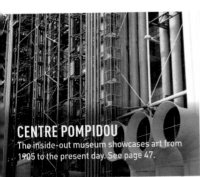

CENTRE POMPIDOU
The inside-out museum showcases art from 1905 to the present day. See page 47.

ARC DE TRIOMPHE
Built to celebrate Napoleon's victories, it dominates the Champs-Élysées. See page 58.

EIFFEL TOWER
Built for the 1889 World Fair, it is still the most potent symbol of Paris. See page 80.

THE MARAIS
Atmospheric streets, museums, trendy bars, and some of the city's finest architecture. See page 50.

JARDIN DU LUXEMBOURG
The perfect Parisian park. See page 76.

THE LOUVRE
Once the home of kings, now home to the world's most outstanding art collection. See page 37.

MONTMARTRE
Artistic heritage, lively bars and some of the most romantic streets in the city. See page 64.

PLACE DES VOSGES
One of Paris' most lovely squares. See page 53.

NOTRE-DAME
A monument to Catholicism and the skill of the great Gothic architects. See page 28.

MUSÉE D'ORSAY
A treasure trove of Impressionist works. See page 78.

A PERFECT DAY

8.00am

Breakfast
If your hotel doesn't serve breakfast, ask the concierge for directions to the nearest good *boulangerie*; buy some freshly-baked croissants or *pains au chocolat* and find a leafy square nearby to eat them in.

11.00am

Coffee break
At the Palais du Luxembourg, turn left and walk along the railings of the famous Jardin du Luxembourg, the most elegant of Paris's parks. Stop for a strong espresso at smart café Le Rostand (see page 114), on the square at the garden's eastern tip.

9.00am

Seine boat tour
Begin at the city's origin, the River Seine. Make your way to the western tip of the Île de la Cité, via the steps down from Pont-Neuf. From here, take one of the Vedettes du Pont-Neuf boat tours; it is a lovely way to see the city.

10.30am

Rue de Seine
From Pont-Neuf, walk along quai de Conti, then amble down characterful rue de Seine with its art and fashion boutiques.

12 noon

Park and lunch
After a stroll through the Jardin du Luxembourg among joggers, *boules* players and smooching couples, make your way to nearby restaurant La Ferrandaise (see page 114) and enjoy a nice light lunch of updated French classics.

IN **PARIS**

4.30pm

Retail therapy
Make your way back to Métro St-Paul and go straight to Charles-de-Gaulle-Étoile station. Take a moment outside the station to admire the Arc de Triomphe (see page 58), then walk down the Champs-Élysées, dipping into the swanky, big-brand shops as you go.

9.30pm

Bar hopping
Walk downhill to boulevard de Rochechouart and take a taxi to the République and Oberkampf area, which is littered with trendy bars. Try rue Jean-Pierre Timbaud, which runs parallel to rue Oberkampf, just east of place de la République – the perfect counterpoint to the historic attractions you saw earlier.

2.00pm

Paris history
Walk towards the river along teeming boulevard St-Michel, then catch the Métro to St-Paul. Walk up rue Malher to the Musée Carnavalet (see page 51) and spend an hour or two exploring Paris's history through the paintings and artefacts.

6.00pm

Montmartre and dinner
Take the Métro to Abbesses, on the hill of Montmartre. Follow your nose through the atmospheric, winding streets. After a relaxed bistro dinner at Chez Toinette (see page 113), walk to Sacré-Cœur and savour the panoramic view over the city from its front steps.

CONTENTS

INTRODUCTION

It's hard to argue with Victor Hugo's description of Paris as 'the city of cities'. For over 2,000 years, it has steadily grown in size and reputation, and each of its many layers is rich in history and intrigue. Unlike many European cities, it was left almost unscathed by the two world wars, and its celebrated streets, monuments and museums still work their centuries-old magic today. And then there's the artistic heritage of the 'City of Light'; long a powerhouse of art, literature, music and philosophy. Little wonder that the Parisians are so proud to be part of a city that, according to writer Jean Giraudoux, has been home to, 'the greatest amount of thinking, talking and writing in the world'.

GEOGRAPHY

Paris centres around the River Seine, whose flowing waters have long been the lifeblood of the city. The River Seine enters Paris close to the Bois de Vincennes in the southeast and meanders gently north and south past three small, heavily developed islands – the Île St-Louis, Île de la Cité and, on its way out, Île des Cygnes. Chains of hillocks add perspective to the city, with Montmartre (the city's highest point), Ménilmontant, Belleville and Buttes Chaumont rising up to the north of the river, and to the south, Montsouris, the Mont Ste-Geneviève, Buttes aux Cailles and Maison Blanche.

At the beginning of the 19th century, Napoleon imposed a special status on the city of Paris, giving it the powers of a *département* in order to maintain a firm hold on the capital's politics and populace. Today, each *arrondissement* also has its own council and mayor to deal with local affairs. In the two houses of the French Parliament, 21 delegates and 12 senators represent the city.

THE RIVER

Fluctuat nec mergitur ('[She] is tossed by the waves but does not sink'), reads the Latin inscription on the capital's coat-of-arms, symbolising a city born beside the River Seine. Today, the Seine

Parisian facades

cuts a swathe through the city's middle and is the capital's widest avenue, spanned by a total of 37 bridges, which provide some of the loveliest views of Paris.

The river is the city's calmest thoroughfare, notwithstanding the daily flow of tourist and commercial boat traffic. In the 19th century, the banks were encumbered with wash-houses and watermills, and its waters heaved with ships from every corner of France. More difficult to imagine are the 700 Viking warships that sailed up the river to invade Paris in the 9th century. Today, barges and pleasure boats ply the river, some on their way to Burgundy via the St-Martin and St-Denis canals, which cut across the north-east of the city.

PARIS AMBIENCE

One of the most persistent images of Paris is of long avenues elegantly lined with chestnut and plane trees. Flowers and plants abound in a patchwork of squares, parks and gardens, tended in the formal French tradition, or following the English style so admired by Napoleon III. Divided up by two long ribbons of streets, one tracing a long line north to south (from boulevard de Strasbourg to boulevard St-Michel) and the other running from east to west (from rue du Faubourg-St-Antoine as far as La Défense), Paris is a mosaic of *quartiers* (quarters) or 'villages', each with a distinctive character.

The most important, unofficial division in Paris is between the traditionally working-class eastern end of the city and the mostly bourgeois west. In general, the further east you go, the further left you will find yourself on the political spectrum. Rents are steep in the western *arrondissements*, whereas

⊙ CAFÉ CULTURE

Cafés have long played a key part in the city's intellectual, political and artistic development. Café Voltaire (1 place de l'Odéon) was where, in the 18th century, Voltaire used to meet fellow philosopher Diderot to discuss their Enlightenment theories. The 19th-century poets Verlaine and Mallarmé also conversed here, and in the 1920s the American writers Ernest Hemingway and F. Scott Fitzgerald extolled the café's 'sudden provincial quality'. Between the two world wars, other writers in Paris spent hours at their favourite tables in Le Procope (13 rue de l'Ancienne-Comédie), while the Existentialist writer and philosopher Jean-Paul Sartre and his lover Simone de Beauvoir consolidated the highbrow reputation of Les Deux Magots (6 place St-Germain-des-Prés) in the 1950s.

property is less expensive, though hardly affordable, in the east. City planners have been struggling for decades to improve the balance, culminating in massive urban renewal projects at Bercy and the 'new' Left Bank: Paris Rive Gauche (see page 74) in the southeast.

Legendary Left-Bank Café de Flore

POPULATION

Paris is more densely populated than Tokyo, London or New York. At odds with the city's spacious boulevards, Parisians live literally on top of one another, squeezed into small apartments, packed into the city's 100 sq km (40 sq miles). A house or a garden are almost unheard-of luxuries. There is intense competition for desirable living space, with an average of 150,000 people looking for a home at any one time. It is an oft-cited paradox that this battle for a place to live occurs in a city where 26 percent of apartments lie vacant. High rents can mean that many Parisians have neither the time nor the money to appreciate the city they live in, being trapped in a monotonous routine they describe as *Métro-boulot-dodo* (commuting, working, sleeping).

Nonetheless, for anyone fortunate enough to live in the city centre, the rewards far outweigh the demands. Human in scale, cosmopolitan and lively, Paris lives up to its reputation as one of the best cities on earth for enjoying the good life.

A BRIEF HISTORY

Paris began as an island fishing community and trading port in the middle of the River Seine. Stone Age inhabitants left some of the earliest traces (4500BC) on the Right Bank under what is now Bercy, but it was c.250BC before the town took form under the skilful hands of the Parisii. According to the Greek geographer Strabo, the Celtic tribe built their main city on the largest island on the river, presumably the Île de la Cité. The island, well away from the banks of the river – much wider than today – may well have provided refuge from the fierce Belgae to the east. The Parisii minted their own finely crafted gold coins for trade as far afield as Britain and the Mediterranean, and the town's prosperity and strategic position attracted the attention of Julius Caesar, whose legions conquered it in 52BC.

According to some philologists, the town's Gallo-Roman name of Lutetia means 'marshland', reflecting the character of the land that then bordered the river. The Romans built their settlement just above the flood plain, on what is now the Left Bank's Latin Quarter. Rue St-Jacques and rue St-Martin follow the route of the old Roman road linking northern France to Orléans. Scant subterranean masonry has been found from the Roman buildings – forum, theatres, temples – but there are

Places of worship

France has no official state religion, but the sway of the Catholic Church during the nation's long history is still very much in evidence. As well as its many Catholic churches, Paris has a long list of places of worship dedicated to other varieties of Christianity and other faiths, notably Judaism, Islam and Hinduism.

substantial remains of the public baths in what is now a wing of the Musée National du Moyen Age.

Huns and Franks over-ran Roman Gaul in the 3rd century, driving the citizens to retrench in the fortified Île de la Cité, which was renamed Paris around this time. In 508, Clovis, King of the Franks, set up court here. He later converted to Christianity, and several religious foundations date from this time, including those of the city's oldest church, St-Germain-des-Prés.

Clovis, King of the Franks

THE CAPETIANS

Norman pirates regularly raided Paris from AD 845 onwards. The city stagnated until 987, when Hugues Capet, Count of Paris, became King of France. His Capetian dynasty went on to make the city the economic and political capital of France. The River Seine was once again the key to commercial prosperity, symbolised by the ship on the city's coat-of-arms. The Right Bank port area, known as the Grève, developed around the site of the present-day Hôtel de Ville.

Philippe Auguste (1180–1223) used the revenue from trade to build the Louvre fortress (its lower ramparts are clearly visible beneath today's museum), Notre-Dame Cathedral, paved streets, aqueducts and freshwater fountains. To protect his investment while he was away on the Third Crusade, he surrounded the city with walls.

The profoundly devout, and later canonised, Louis IX (1226–70) gave the city one of its great Gothic masterpieces, Sainte-Chapelle. His patronage of spiritual and intellectual life also gave rise to the learned character of the modern day Latin Quarter. The Sorbonne University evolved from the many new schools established here, frequented in their day by Latin-speaking clerics and established by the king's chaplain, Robert de Sorbon. By the end of Louis's reign, Paris was one of the largest cities in Western Christendom, with a population of 100,000.

In the 14th century, the city's merchant class took advantage of the political vacuum left by the devastating Black Death and the Hundred Years War with England. In 1356, with King Jean le Bon held prisoner at Poitiers, Etienne Marcel – the merchants' leader – set up a municipal government in Paris. Although he was assassinated two years later, he had shown that the Parisians were a force to be reckoned with. Wary of their militancy, Jean's successor Charles V built the formidable Bastille fortress.

ENGLISH RULE AND RELIGIOUS CONFLICT

Civil unrest continued unabated. In 1407 – during the second phase of the Hundred Years War between England and France – the Duke of Burgundy had the Duke of Orléans assassinated on rue Barbette, which led to 12 years of strife between their supporters. The Burgundians allied themselves with the English, who entered Paris in 1420, following the French defeat at Agincourt under Henry V, the English King. Henry had just signed the Treaty of Troyes with King Charles VII of France, which made him Regent and his son, Henry VI, King of England and France, at nine months old. Charles VII retained vast territories in central and southern France and, ten years after Troyes, Joan of Arc was able to lead the French army to several important victories in France, while England was divided by its nobles' interests. The Treaty of Arras (1435) between Charles VII and Henry's former ally, Philip III of Burgundy, brought the dual monarchy to an end. Charles VII reclaimed Paris in 1436 and by 1453 the English Monarchy had lost all its possessions in France, save Calais.

In the early 16th century, Paris thrived under an absolutist and absent monarch, François I (1515–47), who was occupied with wars in Italy, and even imprisoned for a year in Spain. Much of the Louvre was torn down and rebuilt along the present lines. A new Hôtel de Ville (city hall) was begun, as well as the grand St-Eustache church.

The new splendour was soon bloodied by religious war, starting in 1572 with the St Bartholomew's Day massacre of 3,000 Protestants in Paris and culminating in the siege of the city by Henri de Navarre in 1589. Before the Catholic League capitulated, 13,000 Parisians had died of starvation. Henri was crowned at Chartres and finally entered the capital in 1594 – not before having converted to Catholicism himself, though his quip, 'Paris is well worth a Mass' is almost certainly apocryphal.

Henri IV did Paris proud once he was its master. He built the beautiful place des Vosges and place Dauphine, embellished the banks of the river with the quai de l'Arsenal, quai de l'Horloge

Louis XVI faces the guillotine

and quai des Orfèvres, and even constructed the Samaritaine hydraulic machine that pumped fresh water to Right Bank households until 1813. The most popular of France's monarchs, *le bon roi Henri* (good King Henry) was a notorious ladies' man. He completed the Pont-Neuf (the oldest bridge in Paris), as well as the adjacent gardens, where he was known to dally with his ladies.

During the reign of Louis XIII (1610–43), Paris began to take on the fashionable aspect that became its hallmark. Elegant houses sprang up along rue du Faubourg-St-Honoré, and the magnificent *hôtels* (mansions) of the nobility were constructed in the Marais. The capital strengthened its hold on the country with the founding of a royal printing press and Cardinal Richelieu's Académie Française.

Paris increasingly attracted nobles from the provinces – although too many for the liking of Louis XIV, *le Roi Soleil* ('the Sun King', 1643–1715). To bring his overly powerful and independent aristocrats into line, Louis decided to move the court out to Versailles, compelling the courtiers to live at ruinous expense in his enormous new palace.

Paris lost some of its political importance, but looked more impressive than ever, with the landscaping of the Jardin des Tuileries and the Champs-Élysées, and the building of the Louvre's great colonnade and the Invalides hospital for wounded soldiers.

The city asserted a leading cultural position in Europe with its new academies of the arts, literature and sciences and the establishment of the Comédie Française (1680) and several other theatres.

The rumble of popular discontent grew louder however, as corruption and heavy taxes for costly foreign wars marked the reigns of the Sun King's successors, the languid Louis XV (1715–74) and the inept Louis XVI (1774–93). One of the final construction projects of the *ancien régime* was a 23km (14 mile) wall encircling the city. Begun in 1784, it was a key factor in the subsequent unrest, for at points along the wall taxes were collected on goods brought into the city.

THE REVOLUTION

Paris was the epicentre of the political earthquake that was the French Revolution, whose aftershocks spread across France to shake up a whole continent. It started with protests about taxes, but turned into an assault on the privileges of the monarchy, the aristocracy and the church. Middle-class intellectuals made common cause with the urban poor, the previously powerless *sans-culottes* (literally, people without breeches). The revolutionaries destroyed the prison-fortress of the Bastille on 14 July 1789, and proceeded to execute the perceived enemies of the new republic.

A climax was reached on 21 January 1793, with the public beheading of Louis XVI. In the Reign of Terror later that year, several revolutionaries followed Louis to the guillotine: Camille Desmoulins, the fiery orator; Danton, who tried to moderate the Terror; and then the men who had organised it, Robespierre and Saint-Just.

FIRST EMPIRE

In 1799, Napoleon Bonaparte became first consul, and later made himself emperor. For Paris, he performed all the functions of an enthusiastic mayor, scarcely hindered by his military expeditions abroad. Detailed maps of Paris and architectural plans for new buildings were always part of his baggage. For all his spectacular monuments – the Arc de Triomphe is one example – the emperor was proudest of his civic improvements: better fresh water supplies, improved drainage, new food markets and a streamlined municipal administration and police force. Most of his reforms survived long after his final defeat in 1815.

THE RESTORATION

Although the monarchy was restored in 1814, it faced an ever-present threat in Paris from dissatisfied workers, radical intellectuals and a highly ambitious bourgeoisie. In July 1830 protest turned to riots and the building of barricades. Charles X was forced to abdicate. However, instead of restoring the republic, the revolutionary leaders played it safe and accepted the moderate Louis-Philippe, the so-called 'Citizen King'.

The Revolution of 1848, which brought Louis-Philippe's monarchy to an end, likewise started with riots and barricades in the streets of Paris. A mob threatened the royal palace, forcing the king to flee; they then invaded the Chamber of Deputies, demanding a republic. Elections followed, but they showed that however radical Paris might be, the rest of France was still largely conservative. The new National Assembly withdrew the concessions that had been made to the workers, and up went the

Guillotine bridge

Masonry from the Bastille was used to build the bridge leading to what was then the place de la Révolution – now place de la Concorde – where the guillotine was erected.

barricades again. This time the army was called in with its heavy guns. At least 1,500 insurrectionists were killed, and thousands deported.

SECOND EMPIRE

The democratically-elected president, Louis-Napoleon (a nephew of Napoleon Bonaparte, whose son had died young), seized absolute power in 1851 and the following year became

Napoleon Bonaparte

Emperor Napoleon III. Fear led him to modernise Paris. The insurrections of 1830 and 1848 had flared up in the densely populated working-class districts around the centre, and he wanted to prevent a recurrence. He commissioned Baron Georges Haussmann to do away with the narrow and insalubrious alleys that nurtured discontent, and moved the occupants to the suburbs. The city was opened up with broad avenues; these so-called *grands boulevards* were too wide for barricades and gave the artillery a clear line of fire in case of revolt.

The Second Empire was a time of joyous abandon and expansion, but the emperor stumbled into war against Prussia in 1870. The army was quickly defeated, and Napoleon III's disgrace and capture brought the proclamation of a new republic, followed by a crippling Prussian siege of Paris. The city held out, albeit reduced to starvation level. When France's leaders agreed to peace, there was another uprising.

THIRD AND FOURTH REPUBLICS

The Paris Commune, the surprisingly moderate and efficient rule of an elected revolutionary council, lasted 10 weeks, from 18 March to 29 May 1871, until Adolphe Thiers, the first president of the Third Republic, sent in troops from Versailles to crush it. In the last days, the *communards* set fire to the Palais des Tuileries and executed hostages. At least 20,000 Commune supporters were executed in retaliation.

Prosperity rapidly returned, marked by a great construction boom. Projects begun under Napoleon III, such as the Palais-Garnier and the huge Les Halles market, were finished. The city showed off its new face at the 1889 World Fair, with the Eiffel Tower as its monumental centrepiece. The splendid Métro system was inaugurated in 1900.

After this period of peace, however, two wars took their toll. The Germans failed to take Paris during World War I, but occupied it for four years during World War II. The city escaped heavy bombing, and Hitler's vengeful order to destroy the city before retreating was ignored. Liberation came eventually, with a grand parade down the Champs-Élysées by General Charles de Gaulle, his Free French forces and US and British allies.

The post-war city regained its cultural lustre under the influence of figures such as Camus, Sartre, Juliette Gréco and bebop musicians. Under a rapid succession of governments, however, economic recovery was slow.

FIFTH REPUBLIC

The Fourth Republic collapsed in 1958 after an army revolt during the colonial war in Algeria. Recalled from retirement, de Gaulle became the first president of the Fifth Republic and set about the task of restoring French prestige and morale.

FROM THE 1968 RIOTS TO MITTERRAND'S PRESIDENCY

Barricades and insurrection hit Paris again in May 1968. With workers on strike, students hurled the Latin Quarter's paving stones at the Establishment. However, national elections showed that Paris was once more at odds with most of France, which voted for stability. Succeeding de Gaulle, Georges Pompidou

General Charles de Gaulle

affirmed the new prosperity with controversial riverside expressways and skyscrapers, and the striking Beaubourg cultural centre that bears his name.

In 1977 Jacques Chirac became the first democratically-elected mayor of Paris in over a century. Although critics disapproved of his shopping mall that replaced the old markets of Les Halles, Chirac is credited with cleaning up the formerly dirty streets.

President François Mitterrand (1981–95) made his mark on the Paris skyline with a series of imposing works (his *grands projets*): the pyramid centrepiece of the reorganised Louvre, the Grande Arche de La Défense, the Opéra Bastille, the Institut du Monde Arabe and the national library that bears his name.

PARIS TODAY

Chirac became president in 1995. However, within two years his popularity had dwindled, and the Socialist leader Lionel Jospin became prime minister. Their period of joint stewardship was one of economic growth, reduced unemployment and rising property values. In 2001 Bertrand Delanoë became the city's first Socialist mayor for 130 years. Although Chirac beat the National Front candidate Jean-Marie Le Pen in the 2002 presidential election, the support for Le Pen was shocking. In his second term, President Chirac led a determined opposition to the war in Iraq, which saw his ratings soar, only to plummet after initiating reforms to the state pension and benefit system. His party's candidate to succeed him, Nicolas Sarkozy, won the presidency in May 2007 with promises of sweeping economic and social reforms. His 'Grand Paris' scheme, which aimed to make the city and its suburbs a single administrative unit, saw improved transport links and the construction of landmark skyscrapers. However, he so alienated voters with his fondness for luxury that in 2012 François Hollande became the first Socialist president since François Mitterrand. In April 2014, Anne Hidalgo was elected the first female mayor.

In January 2015, 12 people were killed and 11 injured in an attack by the so-called Islamic State on the Paris headquarters of the satirical magazine, *Charlie Hebdo*. Hundreds of thousands of people participated in marches against terrorism. However, Islamist extremists struck again, killing 130 people and injuring hundreds more in a series of attacks across the city on 13 November. In the 2017 presidential election, relative newcomer and leader of the En Marche! "radical centrist" party, Emmanuel Macron, swept to victory against Marine Le Pen's extreme far-right Front National and became the youngest head of state since Napoleon. Whether he can fulfil his promise to introduce radical economic reforms remains to be seen, but the political establishment has certainly been shaken up. The tentatively optimistic mood in France blossomed into full-blown joy when, in July 2018, it won the FIFA World Cup.

HISTORICAL LANDMARKS

c.250 BC Celtic settlement in the Paris area.

52 BC Roman conquest and founding of Lutetia on the Left Bank.

508 Clovis, King of the Franks, makes Paris his capital.

987 Hugues Capet elected King of France.

1431 Henry VI of England crowned King of France.

1594 Henri IV enters Paris.

1789 Storming of Bastille starts French Revolution.

1793 Execution of Louis XVI and Marie-Antoinette; Reign of Terror.

1804 Napoleon Bonaparte becomes emperor.

1814–15 Fall of Napoleon; restoration of Bourbon monarchy.

1848 Revolution brings Louis-Napoleon to power.

1870–1 Franco-Prussian War; Second Empire ends; Paris besieged.

1871 Paris Commune – 10 weeks of workers' rule.

1900 First Métro line opened.

1914–18 World War I. Germans advance to within eight miles of Paris.

1939 World War II begins.

1940 French government capitulates; Germans occupy Paris.

1944 Free French and other Allied forces liberate Paris.

1958 Fall of Fourth Republic. De Gaulle becomes president.

1968 Student riots, workers' general strikes.

1977 Jacques Chirac becomes first elected mayor since 1871.

1981 President Mitterrand elected president.

1995 Jacques Chirac elected president.

2002 The euro replaces the franc as France's unit of currency.

2007 Nicolas Sarkozy elected president.

2012 Socialist François Hollande elected president.

2014 Socialist Anne Hidalgo is elected Paris's first female mayor.

2015 In January, Islamic terrorists attack at *Charlie Hebdo* kill 12 people; in November, a further series of attacks kill 130 people.

2017 Emmanuel Macron wins the Presidential election.

2018 France wins the FIFA World Cup. French protests take place over higher living costs and fuel tax.

Place de la Concorde and the Eiffel
Tower

WHERE TO GO

Paris is a compact and logically-ordered city that anyone can quickly get the hang of. Its public transport networks are highly efficient, but by far the best way to get to know the city is to potter around it on foot, allowing plenty of time for aimless but often fruitful digressions. The river creates the main division, and the Right Bank (Rive Droite) and Left Bank (Rive Gauche) have their distinct, long-established associations. Right has the reputation as the powerhouse of business and commerce; Left is the historic centre of learning. There is also a traditional east-west divide between the wealthy west and poorer, more radical east. But even these boundaries are porous, and arty centres of creativity are now more likely to be in the northeast of the city than in affluent St-Germain-des-Prés, and young urban professionals are increasingly buying into the traditionally working class parts of the city.

Administratively, the city is divided into 20 *arrondissements*, starting with the 1st in the centre (taking in Île de la Cité and the area around the Louvre) and spiralling outwards clockwise to end at the 20th in the northeast. Confusingly, while Parisians often refer to the *arrondissement* in which they live, they also refer to the historic *quartiers,* such as the Marais, Bastille or Latin Quarter, that often straddle *arrondissements* (the Marais, for example, extends into the 3rd and the 4th *arrondissements*; the Latin Quarter into the 5th and 6th).

ÎLE DE LA CITÉ

The Île de la Cité has long been the heart of Paris. During the 3rd century BC, the Celtic Parisii tribe are thought to have set up home on this, the largest island in the Seine. In 52BC, Roman legions conquered the settlement and founded Lutetia Parisiorum on the left bank. During the Middle Ages, the island was the centre of political, religious and judicial power, not only for Paris but for the whole of France. Nowadays, it is still the geographical centre of the capital and home to several of the city's main official buildings. Sainte-Chapelle and Notre-Dame also make the island an enduring focus for religious tourism.

NOTRE-DAME

Dominating the island is **Notre-Dame ❶** (www.notredame deparis.fr; Mon–Fri 8am–6.45pm; Sat–Sun 8am–7.15pm; free guided tours in English Mon, Tues & Sat 2.30pm, Wed-Fri 2.00pm). The site has played a religious role for at least 2,000 years. In Roman times a temple to Jupiter stood here; in the 4th century AD it was replaced by a Christian church, St-Etienne; this was joined two centuries later by a second church, dedicated to the Virgin. Norman raids left them both in a sorry state, and, in the 12th century, Bishop Maurice de Sully decided that a cathedral should be built to replace them.

The main part of Notre-Dame, begun in 1163, took 167 years to finish. Its transition from Romanesque to Gothic has been called a perfect representation of medieval architecture – an opinion that has provoked some dissent. Cistercian monks protested that such a sumptuous structure was an insult to the godly virtue of poverty, and today some architectural purists still find Notre-Dame excessive.

The original architect is unknown, but Pierre de Montreuil (who was involved in the building of Sainte-Chapelle, see page 32) was responsible for much of the 13th-century work. The present look of the cathedral is due to Eugène Viollet-le-Duc, who from 1845 to 1863 restored it to repair the ravages of the 18th century, caused more by pre-Revolutionary meddlers than by revolutionaries stripping it of religious symbols. Popular support for the expensive restoration was inspired by Victor Hugo's novel, *Notre-Dame de Paris*.

The cathedral has witnessed numerous momentous occasions over the centuries, including, in 1239, the procession of Louis IX, during which the pious king walked barefoot, carrying his holy treasure – believed to be Christ's crown of thorns. In 1594 Henri IV made his politically-motivated conversion to Catholicism here to reinforce his hold on the French throne. Napoleon crowned himself emperor at Notre-Dame, upstaging the Pope, who had come to Paris expecting to do it; the scene is depicted in Jacques-Louis David's vast painting, *The Consecration of Napoleon,* now in the Louvre. Other occasions include General de Gaulle marking the

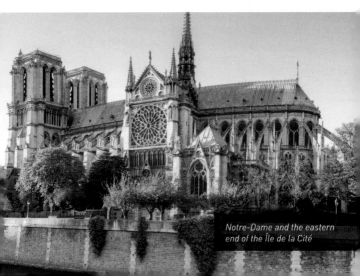

Notre-Dame and the eastern end of the Île de la Cité

View of Conciergerie

1944 Liberation of Paris with a Mass here, and in 1970 his death was also commemorated here.

THE WEST FRONT

Across the three doorways of the west front, the 28 statues of the **Galerie des Rois** represent the kings of Judah. These are 19th-century restorations: the originals were torn down during the Revolution because they were thought to depict kings of France. Twenty-one of them were discovered in 1977 and moved to the Musée du Moyen Age (see page 70).

The central **rose window** depicts the Redemption after the Fall. Two more outsized rose windows illuminate the transept; the northern one retains most of its 13th-century glass. A 14th-century *Virgin and Child* is to the right of the choir entrance.

The 255-step climb up the **north tower** (www.monuments-nationaux.fr; daily Apr–Sept 10am–6.30pm, Oct–Mar

10am–5.30pm, until 11pm weekends July–Aug) is rewarded with glorious views of Paris and close-ups of the roof and Notre-Dame's famous gargoyles. Cross over to the south tower to see the 17th-century 13-ton tenor bell, Emmanuel, which was joined by a new tenor bell, Marie, in 2013; eight new bells were installed in the north tower at the same time. There are spectacular views from here too. Napoleon III's town planner Baron Haussmann greatly enlarged the *parvis*, or cathedral forecourt, increasing the impact of the towering west front. Excavations beneath the square have revealed walls and foundations from the Gallic, Roman and medieval eras, which now form part of an exhibition on early Paris. A copper marker set into the ground, known as the *kilomètre zéro*, is the point from which all distances from Paris to the rest of France are measured.

PALAIS DE LA CITÉ

The other architectural and historical highlight on the Île de la Cité is the **Palais de la Cité**, the complex of buildings that includes the Conciergerie, Sainte-Chapelle and the Palais de Justice, the headquarters of the French supreme court.

PALAIS DE JUSTICE

The imposing neoclassical **Palais de Justice** (www.ca-paris. justice.fr; Mon–Fri 9.00am–5.00pm; free), heart of the French legal system, stands on the site of the Roman palace where Emperor Julian was crowned in AD 360. The lobby (Salle des Pas Perdus) is well worth a visit to catch a glimpse of the lawyers, plaintiffs, witnesses, court reporters and hangers-on.

The Conciergerie

Adjacent is the **Conciergerie** ❷ (www.monuments-nationaux. fr; daily 9.30am–6pm), which became a state prison in 1370.

War memorial

Behind Notre-Dame is the Mémorial des Martyrs de la Déportation (www.chemins dememoire.gouv.fr; Tue–Sun Apr–Sept 10am–7pm, Oct–Mar until 5pm; free), a poignant memorial dedicated to the 200,000 French deported to concentration camps during World War II.

The 'medieval' facade is misleading; it dates from the 1850s. The building's greatest notoriety dates from the late 18th century: in 1793, at the height of the Terror, the Conciergerie became the antechamber of the guillotine, with around 2,500 prisoners spending their last night here (see page 19). It is now a museum to its bloody past, displaying items including a guillotine blade, the crucifix before which Marie-Antoinette prayed while captive here, and the lock used on Robespierre's cell. Look out on the Cour des Femmes, where husbands, wives and lovers were allowed a final tryst before the tumbrels came to carry off the prisoners.

Sainte-Chapelle

Concealed in the courtyard between the Palais de Justice and the Conciergerie is the magnificent Gothic **Sainte-Chapelle** ❸ (www.monuments-nationaux.fr; daily Oct–Mar 9am–5pm, Apr–Sept 9am–7pm). The chapel was constructed in 1248 to designs by Pierre de Montreuil to house holy relics, fragments of which were believed to be Christ's Crown of Thorns, bought by the pious King Louis IX (later St-Louis). The lower chapel, with its star-patterned ceiling, was used by palace servants. More impressive is the upper level, where light blazes through 15m (45ft) high glass windows separated by buttresses so slim that there seems to be no wall at all. Of the 1,134 individual pieces of glass, 720 are 13th-century originals.

Between 1789 and 1815 Sainte-Chapelle served various roles: as a flour warehouse in the Revolution, as a club for high-ranking dandies, then as an archive for Napoleon's Consulate. This latter role fortunately saved the chapel from projected destruction, since the bureaucrats could not think of another site in which to keep their mountains of paper.

OTHER ATTRACTIONS ON THE ÎLE DE LA CITÉ

Towards the western end of the island is the pretty, tree-shaded **square du Vert-Galant** and, beyond it, a statue of Henri IV and the restored **Pont-Neuf**, which, despite its name – 'New Bridge' – is the oldest bridge in Paris. The bridge owes its survival to its solid stone – rather than wood – construction, and it was the first bridge in Paris to be constructed

Exquisite stained-glass in Sainte-Chapelle

without houses on it. In 1985, the Pont-Neuf hit the headlines when Bulgarian-born American artist Christo wrapped the entire structure in fabric.

At the eastern end of the island is the colourful **Marché aux Fleurs** on place Louis Lépine, opposite the Préfecture de Police and Hôtel Dieu. The latter, now a hospital, was built on the site of a medieval hospital; it was the scene of intense battles when the police rose up against the occupying Germans in 1944. In contrast to these forbidding structures, the market is an array of small glasshouses selling flowers and plants. On Sunday, the stalls become a market for caged birds.

ÎLE ST-LOUIS

The pedestrianised Pont St-Louis crosses from the Île de la Cité to the **Île St-Louis ❹**, an island renowned for its elegant, exclusive and astronomically expensive mansions. From the western end of the shady quai d'Orléans (at the western end of the island) there is a wonderful view of the apse of Notre-Dame. However, some pilgrims to this spot are more intent on a visit to another Parisian institution: ice-cream parlour **Berthillon** (www.berthillon.fr; Wed–Sun 10am–8pm), at 29–31 rue St-Louis-en-l'Île, the street that cuts through the island. It is a pretty road, dotted with boutiques and restaurants. Towards the eastern end is the baroque church of **St-Louis-en-l'Île** (www.saintlouisenlile.catholique.fr; Mon–Sat 9.30am–1pm, 2–7.30pm, Sun 9am–1pm and 2–7pm), notable for its fine collection of Dutch, Flemish and Italian 16th and 17th century art.

On the northeastern end of the island, at 17 quai d'Anjou, is the grand **Hôtel Lauzun**. Built in 1640 by Louis Le Vau, architect to Louis XIV, it is now owned by the City of Paris. It was here that the poets Théophile Gautier and Charles Baudelaire lived in 1845, and where Baudelaire wrote part of *Les Fleurs du Mal*. It currently houses the Paris Institute of Advanced Studies (www.paris-iea.fr). In the **Hôtel Lambert**, on the corner of rue St-Louis-en-l'Île, Voltaire enjoyed a tempestuous love affair with the lady of the house, the Marquise du Châtelet.

On the island's south bank is the small **Musée Adam Mickiewicz** (by reservation only Wed–Sat 2.15–6pm, tel: 01 55 42 83 85). A Polish poet, Mickiewicz (1798–1855) lived in Paris from 1832 to 1840 and devoted himself to helping oppressed Poles. The 17th century building in which the museum is housed also includes the Polish Library and displays memorabilia of the Polish composer Frédéric Chopin.

Elegant and exclusive Île St-Louis

THE LOUVRE, TUILERIES & CONCORDE

PALAIS DU LOUVRE

The Louvre was eight centuries in the making, but has retained great architectural harmony nonetheless. It was originally built as a fortress by Philippe Auguste in 1190. When Louis XIV moved his court to Versailles, he abandoned the Louvre to artists and other squatters. The Revolutionaries made it a public museum in 1793. As the home of the *Mona Lisa,* the Louvre drew almost unmanageable crowds, until President Mitterrand ordered its reorganisation in the 1980s. A vast reception area and main entrance was excavated in the forecourt and topped by the iconic glass **Pyramid** designed by Sino-American architect I.M. Pei.

⊙ MAKING THE MOST OF THE MUSEUMS

Entry charges for museums range from around €8–12, with reduced rates for children, students and pensioners. Some museums charge less on Sundays, and entrance is always free on the first Sunday of the month for the following: the Louvre, Musée d'Orsay, Centre Pompidou, Musée de l'Orangerie, Musée Rodin, Musée Picasso and Musée du Moyen Age. **The Paris Museum Pass** (www.parismuseumpass.com) gives entry to over 50 museums and monuments in Paris and its surroundings, including the Louvre and Versailles. You can buy passes valid for two, four or six consecutive days at museums, tourist offices and Métro stations.

MUSÉE DU LOUVRE

The **Musée du Louvre**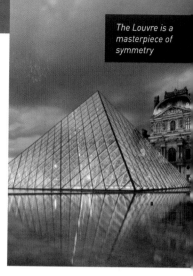
(tel: 01 40 20 53 17; www.
louvre.fr; Wed–Mon 9am–
6pm, Wed and Fri until
9.45pm, tickets valid all day
and allow re-entry into the
museum; free first Sunday
of the month) is divided into
three wings: Richelieu in
the north, Sully in the east
and Denon in the south. The
collections are arranged in
colour-coded sections. A
free map is available at
the ticket desks, where an
audio guide with interactive map can also be rented and the useful official mobile app can be downloaded free.

The Louvre is a masterpiece of symmetry

The following is a summary of the Louvre's many treasures,
including some of the highlights in the different sections.

Lower-Ground and Ground Floors

A good place to start is the exhibition on the medieval
Louvre, on the lower-ground floor of the Sully Wing. This is
where you can see the remains of Philippe-Auguste's fort
and keep, and some of the artefacts discovered in the 1980s
excavations. On the lower ground floor of the Denon Wing
is the Department of Islamic Art, which opened in 2012 and
is recognisable by its iridescent, undulating roof. Above, on
the ground floor of the Sully Wing, are Egyptian and Greek
Antiquities, and on the ground floor of the Denon wing are
Etruscan and Roman antiquities.

The lower ground floor of the Richelieu wing showcases French sculpture, including Guillaume Coustou's giant *Horses of Marly*. The French sculpture collection continues on the ground floor of the Richelieu wing, with works spanning the 5th to 18th centuries. Also here are Mesopotamian finds, such as the black basalt Babylonian *Code of Hammurabi* (1792–1750BC), one of the world's first legal documents.

First and Second Floors

The first floor houses some of the biggest crowd-pullers. The first floor of the Denon Wing is a spectacular collection of large-format French painting, notably Delacroix's *Liberty Leading the People*, Géricault's *Raft of the Medusa* and David's *Consecration of Napoleon*. Adjacent is a room showcasing

Inside the Louvre

Leonardo da Vinci's enigmatic Florentine noblewoman, the *Mona Lisa* (known in French as *La Joconde*). This iconic piece, painted in 1503, is now displayed behind bulletproof glass in a special, frequently crowded room that it shares with Veronese's vast *Wedding at Cana* canvas.

At the staircase dividing the Denon and Sully wings is the *Winged Victory of Samothrace* (2nd century BC), a Hellenistic figurehead commemorating a victory at sea, and the glittering Galerie d'Apollon (Apollo's Gallery), home to the crown jewels. At this point you reach the Sully Wing and the graceful Hellenic statue of the *Venus de Milo* (2nd century BC), bought by the French government for 6,000 francs in 1820 from the island of Milos. Most of the first floor of the Richelieu Wing houses works of the decorative arts.

The whole second floor is dedicated to painting, with high-lights including Dürer's *Self-Portrait*, Vermeer's *The Lacemaker*, Watteau's *Pierrot* and Ingres's *The Turkish Bath*. The Richelieu Wing houses works from Flanders, the Netherlands, Germany and France (14th to 17th centuries); the second floor of the Sully Wing is devoted to French paintings of the 17th, 18th and 19th centuries.

Additional Museums

The Rohan and Marsan wings at 107–111 rue de Rivoli house the **Musée des Arts Décoratifs**, which boasts over 150,000 objects dedicated to the art of French craftsmanship and design, from the Middle Ages to the present day, and the **Library du MAD**, which houses an extraordinary collection of books on the decorative arts, graphic arts, architecture, design, costume and fashion, the history of art and the art of gardening (www.madparis.fr; Tue–Sun 11am–6pm, Thu until 9pm - temporary exhibitions only, audio guide included).

PALAIS-ROYAL

The **Palais-Royal** ⑥ is directly north of the Louvre, across rue de Rivoli. Built in 1639 as Cardinal Richelieu's residence, it gained its regal title when Anne of Austria moved in with young Louis XIV. This serene, arcaded palace has a colourful past. In the days of Philippe d'Orléans, Prince Regent while Louis XV was a child, it was the scene of notorious orgies. A later duke (another Philippe) built apartments above the arcades, along with two theatres (one now the Comédie Française, see page 96), shops, gambling houses and fashionable cafés.

Despite efforts to curry favour with the revolutionaries, such as calling himself Philippe Égalité (equality), the duke ended up on the guillotine with the rest of the family. After the Revolution, the palace became a gambling den again and narrowly escaped destruction during the 1871 uprising. However, following the restoration of the monarchy (1872–76), it regained respectability. The palace now houses the Ministry of Culture, the Council of State, the Constitutional Council, some shops and the historic Grand Véfour restaurant (see page 108).

East of the Palais-Royal is the **Banque de France**, and immediately north is the **Bibliothèque Nationale Richelieu** (www.bnf.fr; Mon–Sat 10am–6pm; free but charge for exhibitions). The latter became a royal library in 1368, when Charles

V placed 973 manuscripts in the Louvre. Most of the millions of books, engravings and ancient manuscripts it has accumulated over the centuries have been transferred to the newer national library on the Left Bank (see page 74). The old building with its splendid reading room (1863) has been transformed into a specialist research library.

THE TUILERIES

West of the Louvre is one of the city centre's main green spaces, the **Jardin des Tuileries** ❼ (daily Apr, May & Sept 7am–9pm, Jun–Aug 7am–11pm, Jan–Mar 7.30am-7.30pm; free), commissioned in 1564 by Catherine de Medici to be the garden for her new Palais des Tuileries. Tuileries were workshops that made roof tiles in the area, before the crown purchased the site and André Le Nôtre landscaped the area. The Palais des Tuileries was the formal home of the French monarchy until its destruction in the upheaval of the Paris Commune in 1871. The current gardens extend across the palace's former site.

Walk around the chestnut and lime trees, and admire sculptor Aristide Maillol's sensual statues of nymphs and languorous maidens, a few of which are coquettishly concealed behind a miniature maze. A project is currently underway to restore the gardens to their original glory and to make them even more welcoming to the 14 million people who visit them each year.

At the eastern entrance to the Tuileries is the pink **Arc de Triomphe du Carrousel**, built by Napoleon at roughly the same time as the Arc de Triomphe. The latter is visible from here in a straight

Cour d'Honneur

In 1986, artist Daniel Buren installed rows of black-and-white-striped stone columns in the Palais-Royal's main quadrangle, the Cour d'Honneur.

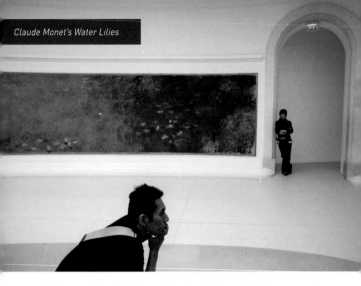
Claude Monet's Water Lilies

line beyond the Obelisk on place de la Concorde. The same axis continues into the distant haze to the skyscrapers of La Défense.

Jeu de Paume and Musée de l'Orangerie

A few surviving fragments of the Palais des Tuileries can be seen by the **Jeu de Paume**, in the northwest corner of the gardens. Once home to real-tennis courts (hence the name) and later to the collection of Impressionist paintings now displayed at the Musée d'Orsay, the building is currently the attractive showcase for the **Centre National de la Photographie** (www.jeudepaume.org; Tue 11am–9pm, Wed–Sun until 7pm). The centre showcases changing exhibitions on all photographic disciplines, including major fashion retrospectives and contemporary video installations.

In the southwest corner of the Tuileries is the **Musée de l'Orangerie** (www.musee-orangerie.fr; Wed–Mon 9am–6pm). The building was originally constructed by Napoleon III to shelter the orange trees of the Jardin des Tuileries, but since the 1920s has been the showcase for eight of Claude Monet's water-lily paintings, the Nymphéas series. In these works, the Impressionist painter captured the play of colour on the pond in his Japanese garden at Giverny (see page 88) at different times of day. Monet and the Louvre's architect drafted the original plans and elevations for their display at the museum. Extensively renovated and reopened in 2006, the two vast oval rooms upstairs still show off the famous paintings to his specification. In the gallery space downstairs is the Jean Walter and Paul Guillaume Collection, an exceptional array of works by artists including Cézanne, Renoir, Matisse, Picasso, Soutine, Modigliani, Utrillo and Henri Rousseau.

PLACE DE LA CONCORDE

In 1753, Ange-Jacques Gabriel designed the vast **place de la Concorde** ❽ as place Louis XV, but the Revolutionaries later dispensed with all royal connotations. The King's statue was replaced with a guillotine, used to behead Louis XVI and over 1,000 other victims. In 1934, the square was the scene of bloody anti-government rioting by French fascists.

In the centre of the square is a pink-granite, 23m (75ft) tall Obelisk, a gift from Mohammed Ali, viceroy of Egypt. Dating from 1300 BC and once part of the temple of Ramses II in Luxor, it was erected here in 1836.

The two horses guarding the entrance to the

Death toll

According to official estimates, 1,119 people were decapitated on place de la Concorde, including Louis XVI, his queen Marie-Antoinette, Charlotte Corday, the poet André Chénier and, ironically, even the Revolutionary leader Robespierre.

Champs-Élysées are replicas of the 18th century *Horses of Marly*, sculpted by Guillaume Coustou (originals are in the Louvre).

THE GRANDS BOULEVARDS

North of the Louvre and Tuileries are the Grand Boulevards, a line of wide avenues running from west to east. The boulevards date from the 17th century, when Louis XIV tore down the medieval walls around Paris and created broad, tree-lined spaces. In the 19th century Baron Haussmann extended the string westwards, and the western end of what was named boulevard Haussmann became the preserve of the rich. High-street clothing chains now dominate stretches of the central boulevards, although traces of Second Empire extravagance can still be seen in the ornate balconies and facades.

PALAIS GARNIER

Dominating the place de l'Opéra is the city's historic opera house, the **Palais Garnier** ❾ (www.operadeparis.fr; daily 10am–5pm; guided tours in English Mon–Sun 11am and 2.30pm, after-hours tours also available), where opera and ballet are performed in tandem with the newer Opéra Bastille (see page 54).

In 1860 architect Charles Garnier was commissioned by Napoleon III to build an opera house. His lavish designs were truly in tune with the pomp and opulence that characterised the Second Empire. A six-ton chandelier dominates the five-tiered auditorium, which is dripping with velvet and gilt. Marc Chagall painted the auditorium ceiling in 1964. Tours also take in the library and museum, showcasing scores, costumes and sets.

MADELEINE

A stock exchange, the Bank of France, a theatre; these were
among the uses proposed for the huge neoclassical church of
La Madeleine (www.eglise-lamadeleine.com; daily 9.30am–
7pm), on place de la Madeleine. Building first began in the 18th
century, but stalled until Napoleon commissioned the current
church in the 19th century as a temple to the glory of his army.
Its colonnaded exterior with a heavily sculpted pediment, emu-
lates a Roman temple such as the Maison Carrée in Nîmes. La
Madeleine's political role was eventually muted when the Arc
de Triomphe was built. The restored monarchy opted to use the
Madeleine as a church, and the building was finally consecrated
in 1842. Climb the steps for great views down rue Royale to
place de la Concorde and the Assemblée Nationale.

Place de la Madeleine is home to luxury food shops, including Fauchon (nicknamed 'millionaire's supermarket') and

The Vendôme column

truffle retailers Maison de la Truffe. Also on the square is the **Kiosque-Théâtre Madeleine** (Tue–Sat 12.30–7.30pm, Sun until 3.45pm), where you can buy half-price seats for same-day theatre shows.

PLACE VENDÔME

Louis XIV wanted this square to be an imposing setting for a monument to him, but after it was laid out in 1699, only his financiers could afford the rent. Today the Ministry of Justice shares the square with banks, jewellers and the Ritz hotel. The statue of Louis XIV was overthrown during the Revolution. Its replacement, the Vendôme column, commemorates the victories of Napoleon and is modelled on Trajan's Column in Rome. Cast from 1,250 Austrian cannons captured at Austerlitz, it is topped by a statue of the emperor. Like him, it was toppled, in the 1871 Commune (see page 22) at the instigation of the painter Gustave Courbet, who had to pay to have it re-erected two years later.

BEAUBOURG, LES HALLES & THE MARAIS

Sandwiched between the Louvre and Palais-Royal to the west and the Marais to the east, Beaubourg and Les Halles form one of the city's busiest commercial and cultural centres. The biggest landmark is the Centre Pompidou, Paris's modern art museum.

For centuries, the Marais district was home to Paris's aristocrats. Today, it is an elegant, characterful district, with fine mansions, museums, attractive boutiques, kosher grocers, gay bars and hip cafés bundled together in a labyrinth of narrow streets.

CHÂTELET AND HÔTEL DE VILLE

Busy Place du Châtelet is a good starting point for exploring the area. Flanked by two theatres (Théâtre de la Ville and Théâtre du Châtelet), the square lies above one of Paris's biggest Métro and RER stations.

Opening out at the eastern end of avenue Victoria is the wide esplanade of the **Hôtel de Ville** ⓫ (Mon–Sat 10am–7pm; free), the ornate home of the city council. The neo-Renaissance building, with its magnificent Mansard roof, was rebuilt after the 17th century town hall was destroyed by fire in the 1871 Commune. In medieval times, place de l'Hôtel de Ville was the site of hangings and executions, but today, the pedestrianised square is considerably more alluring, especially in the evening when the fountains are floodlit. There is an ice-skating rink here in winter.

CENTRE POMPIDOU

'That'll get them screaming,' said then-President Georges Pompidou, as he approved the plans for the cultural centre bearing his name. The **Centre Pompidou** ⓬ (www.centre pompidou.fr; Wed–Mon 11am–9pm, Thu until 11pm - only for exhibitions on level 6) was built by architects Richard Rogers, Renzo Piano and Gianfranco Franchini, and its inside-out design, dominated by external pipes, tubes, scaffolds and escalators, caused controversy when unveiled in 1977. The pipes are not just for show: the blue ones convey air, the green ones carry water, the yellow ones contain the electrics, and the red ones conduct heating.

The building, more popularly known as Beaubourg after its 13th century neighbourhood, houses a cinema, library, design centre, music 'laboratory' and museum. The plaza outside is a popular rendezvous point and the site of the Stravinsky Fountain, featuring colourful sculptures by Niki de Saint Phalle.

One of the world's finest collections of 20th century art, the **Musée National d'Art Moderne** (National Museum of Modern Art) is housed on the fourth and fifth floors, with the fifth floor home to modern works from 1905 to the 1960s, and the fourth floor covering contemporary work from the 1960s to the present day. Highlights of the modern period include works by Kandinsky, Klee, Klein, Matisse, Picasso and Pollock, and sections on Dadaism, Bauhaus and Surrealism. The contemporary collection includes pieces by Andy Warhol, Verner Panton, Joseph Beuys, Gerhard Richter and Jean Dubuffet. On level six are temporary exhibitions and the fashionable, minimalist – and expensive – Georges restaurant (www.beaumarly.com).

Included in the price of the ticket to the Musée National d'Art Moderne is a visit to a reconstruction of sculptor Constantin Brancusi's studio, **Atelier Brancusi** (Wed–Mon 2–6pm; free, closed 1 May).

LES HALLES

For centuries this was the site of the capital's main food market, but to widespread regret, the 19th century iron-and-glass pavilions were demolished in 1971. The market is now located out of town, near Orly. The much disliked partly-subterranean **Forum des Halles** shopping centre took its place, along with its gardens and playgrounds. These were swept away as part of a colossal renovation programme that was completed in 2018. A huge 2.5 hectare (6.2 acre) undulating glass and

The inside-out Centre Pompidou

metal roof (the Canopée) now covers the Chatelet Les Halles métro hub and the Forum shopping mall, which is the largest in Paris, with 127 stores and 22 restaurants, including Champeaux by Alain Ducasse (www.restaurant-champeaux. com). A cultural centre as much as a shopping destination, the complex also includes a library, hip hop centre, rehearsal rooms, an academy of music and a cinema. Near Les Halles is the Renaissance **Fontaine des Innocents**, once part of a cemetery. Bars and restaurants line the adjoining rue Berger and the streets leading off it. Some of the side streets have a seedy feel, and nearby rue St-Denis, once primarily a red-light district, still has a number of sex shops.

The church of **St-Eustache** (Mon–Fri 9.30am–7pm, Sat 10am–7.15pm, Sun 9.15am–7.15pm) dominates the north side of Les Halles. Built from 1532 to 1637, the main structure is late Gothic with an imposing Renaissance colonnade on its western facade. The church stages free organ recitals at 5.30pm on Sundays.

THE MARAIS

This district, to the north of the Île de la Cité and Île St-Louis, has successfully withstood the onslaught of modern construction. It provides a remarkably intact record of the development of the city, from the reign of Henri IV at the end of the 16th century to the advent of the Revolution. Built on reclaimed marshland, as its name suggests (*marais* means 'swamp'), the **Marais** contains some of Europe's most elegant Renaissance mansions (*hôtels*), many of which now serve as museums and libraries. In the 1960s, the government designated the area an historical monument, and conservation and restoration took

The revamped Forum des Halles

hold. The big change in
the last 30 years has been
the steady influx of trendy
boutiques and gay bars.

Take the métro to
Rambuteau and start
at the corner of rue des
Archives and rue des
Francs-Bourgeois, named
after the poor (not bour-
geois at all) who were
allowed to live here tax-
free in the 14th century.
The national archives of
the Ancien Régime are
stored in an 18th-century

Fallafel places in the
Jewish quarter of Le
Marais

mansion, the **Hôtel de Soubise** (Mon, Wed–Fri 10am–5.30pm,
Sat–Sun 2–5.30pm). Across a vast, horseshoe-shaped courtyard, you come across the rococo style of Louis XV's time in the
apartments of the Prince and Princess of Soubise.

A short walk north of here, with its entrance on rue Réaumur,
is the wonderful **Musée des Arts et Métiers** ⓭ (www.arts-et-
metiers.net; Tue–Sun 10am–6pm, Thu until 9.30pm) – nothing, in fact, to do with 'arts and trades', but instead Europe's
oldest science museum. It has a vast collection of treasures
ranging from ancient clocks and barometers to the first ever
steam-powered vehicle, an enormous 1938 TV set and dozens
of vintage cars, all housed in a former Benedictine priory.

A Cluster of Museums

The Marais is home to a number of prestigious museums,
including, on rue des Francs-Bourgeois, the grand **Musée**

Musée Carnavalet

Carnavalet ⑭ (www.car navalet.paris.fr), which charts the history of the city. The museum is housed in the magnificent Hôtel Carnavalet, which was once home to the lady of letters Madame de Sévigné. The museum is closed for renovation until the end of 2019.

Nearby at 5 rue Thorigny, the truly excellent **Musée National Picasso** ⑮ (www.musee picassoparis.fr; Tue–Fri 10.30am–6pm; Sat–Sun from 9.30am) is set within the restored Hôtel Salé. The museum's collections include more than 200 paintings, 158 sculptures and hundreds of drawings, engravings, ceramics and models for stage sets and costumes drawn from the artist's personal collection, as well as works by Braque, Matisse, Miró, Degas, Renoir and Rousseau.

Another Marais museum, housed in the Hôtel Donon at 8 rue Elzévir, is the **Musée Cognacq-Jay** (www.cognacq-jay. paris.fr; Tue–Sun 10am–6pm), which contains a splendid collection of 18th century paintings, furniture and *objets d'art*, bequeathed to the city by the founders of La Samaritaine. This grand old department store (at Châtelet), known for its impressive Art Deco interior, was closed in 2005, ostensibly for safety reasons. The current owner, luxury goods conglomerate LVMH, is converting it into a department store, luxury hotel, Cheval Blanc, as well as 96 social housing units, offices and a crèche.

There are a number of other hôtels of note in the district that are closed to the public (although sometimes open on Heritage Days), but can still be admired from the outside. These include the Hôtel d'Albret, Hôtel d'Aumont and Hôtel de Beauvais. The Hôtel de Sens, the oldest mansion in the Marais, now houses the Bibliothèque Forney and occasionally has exhibitions on the decorative arts that are open to the public, as is the garden. The **Hôtel de Sully** (www.hotel-de-sully.fr) houses the Centre des Monuments Nationaux but the peaceful garden is open to the public (daily 9am–7pm). There is also a library and bookshop (Tue–Sun 1pm–7pm) .

Place des Vosges

Rue des Francs-Bourgeois ends at what many agree is the most attractive residential square in Paris, **place des Vosges** (originally place Royale). Henri IV had it laid out in 1605 on the site of an old horse-market, the idea being to have 'all the houses in the same symmetry'. After the wedding festivities of his son Louis XIII, the gardens became the fashionable place in which to promenade, and later, a spot for aristocratic duels.

The Romantic writer Victor Hugo lived at No. 6, now a **museum** (www. maisonsvictorhugo.paris.

City bike scheme

Since its launch in 2007, the city council's Vélib' automated cycle hire scheme has steadily grown and improved. There are over 1,800 stations across the capital and 30 percent are electric. The bikes are utilitarian but in good working order and prices are reasonable (€5 for 24 hours, no charge for journeys under 30 minutes for regular cycles, €1 for electric cycles). For details, visit www.velib-metropole.fr.

fr; Tue–Sun 10am–6pm) housing a small collection of his artefacts. It is worth visiting to see the interior of one of the square's grand mansions.

Jewish Quarter

As the Marais has become popular with bar and boutique owners, the Jewish community has retreated to a small pocket centred on Rue des Rosiers, which is lined with kosher delis and falafel stands. Jewish history is told at the **Musée d'Art et d'Histoire du Judaïsme** ⓰ (www.mahj.org; Tue–Fri 11am–6pm, Sat and Sun 10am–6pm) on rue du Temple. The **synagogue**, with its Art Nouveau facade by Hector Guimard, is at 4 rue Pavée.

BASTILLE & EASTERN PARIS

For years a run-down area, Bastille was given a shot in the arm by the construction of a new opera house in the late 20th century. The area south of here, Bercy, has since become a potent symbol of urban regeneration, with a disused 19th century railway viaduct and dilapidated wine warehouse district brought back to life and now thriving.

BASTILLE

No trace of the prison stormed in 1789 remains on the **place de la Bastille**. Even the column in the centre commemorates a later revolution, that of 1830. The area was largely ignored, until the **Opéra Bastille** ⓱ (www.operadeparis.fr), one of Mitterrand's *grands projets* (see page 23) was built. Cutting-edge artists and designers, like Jean-Paul Gaultier, moved into the area, and now, in streets such as rue de la Couronne, traditional shops alternate with galleries and cool restaurants. North of the Bastille are rue Oberkampf and rue

Enchanting Place des Vosges

Jean-Pierre Timbaud, where there is a concentration of hip bars and boutiques.

To the south of the Bastille are the quirky shops and cafés of Canal St-Martin, while at 1–129 avenue Daumesnil is the **Viaduc des Arts** (www.leviaducdesarts.com). In the golden age of rail, the Viaduc de Paris, built in 1859, supported a train line from Bastille to the Bois de Vincennes. However, as the railways declined in the 20th century, the viaduct fell into disrepair. It was saved from demolition and reopened in 1998, with attractive glass-fronted workshops, fashion and craft boutiques occupying its arches.

EASTERN PARIS

In **Bercy**, old stone-walled warehouses and cobbled streets have been given a new lease of life in the shape of Bercy Village, centred on cour St-Emilion, home to boutiques, restaurants and cafés. On the north side of the Parc de Bercy, a repurposed Frank Gehry building became the new home of the **Cinémathèque Française**, housing a film museum, research centre, repertory cinema, restaurant and film archive. Pedestrians and cyclists can cross to the Left Bank on the city's newest bridge, the nearby Passerelle Simone de Beauvoir, which opened in 2006.

Also northeast of the Bastille is the colourful neighbourhood of **Belleville**, home to an attractive park with panoramic views of Paris and one of the city's two Chinatowns.

CHAMPS-ÉLYSÉES, TROCADÉRO & WEST

The **Champs-Élysées** ⓲ were designed by landscape architect André Le Nôtre in 1667 as an extension of the Tuileries (see page

⊘ PÈRE LACHAISE CEMETERY

The Cimetière du Père Lachaise (www.pere-lachaise.com; Nov–mid Mar Mon–Fri 8am–5.30pm, Sat 8.30am–5.30pm, Sun 9am–5.30pm, mid Mar–Oct Mon–Fri 8am–6pm, Sat 8.30am–6pm, Sun 9am–6pm) has seen an estimated 1,350,000 burials since its foundation in 1804. It even served as a battleground in 1871, when the Communards made a last stand here: the Mur des Fédérés in the southeast corner marks the place where many of them were executed by firing squad. Tombs of the famous include those of the painter Ingres, dancer Isadora Duncan, composers Rossini and Chopin, and writers such as Molière, Balzac, Proust and Oscar Wilde; the latter honoured with a fine monument by Jacob Epstein. Other famous names include singers Edith Piaf and Jim Morrison, and actress Marie Trintignant.

41). Initially the promenade only reached as far as the Rond-Point des Champs-Élysées, less than half its current length. Over a hundred years passed before the rest of the avenue, stretching up to the Arc de Triomphe, was completed. Its reputation has ebbed and flowed with the centuries, and it is currently experiencing something of a comeback as one of the city's most prestigious shopping strips.

The Champs-Élysées seen from the top of the Arc de Triomphe

CHAMPS-ÉLYSÉES

The commercial stretch of the **Champs-Élysées** runs from the Rond-Point to the Arc de Triomphe. The landmark stores are a four-storey, multi-brand shopping arcade, LE66 (www.le66. fr), at No. 66; Guerlain at No. 68, with its Rococo-style facade and sumptuous interior; Sephora - an Aladdin's cave of beauty products - at No. 70–72; Louis Vuitton at No. 101 and, at No. 53, the Atelier Renault, which has a swish mezzanine restaurant and cocktail bar.

The majority of designer shops are concentrated around avenue Montaigne, the southern end of avenue George V and rue du Faubourg St-Honoré. This is high fashion land, where prices are sky-high.

On the southern side of the Champs, between place Clémenceau and the river, is the imposing, glass-domed **Grand**

Famous macaroons

Renowned in Paris for generations for its delectable macaroons, Ladurée (www.laduree.fr), a bakery/restaurant at 75 avenue des Champs-Élysées, is always busy and very chic. Don't leave without trying the melt-in-the-mouth macaroons, which come in a multitude of flavours. There are other branches in the city.

Palais ⓲ (www.grandpalais.fr; open during exhibitions only, times vary), constructed for the 1900 World Fair. The Grand Palais hosts several major art exhibitions every year; the colossal building also houses the **Palais de la Découverte** (www.palais-decouverte.fr; Tue–Sat 9.30am–6pm, Sun and bank holidays 10am–7pm), which includes a hands-on exhibition of the sciences, with a planetarium as centrepiece.

Across avenue Winston Churchill is the **Petit Palais**, which houses the fine-art collection of the Musée des Beaux-Arts de la Ville de Paris (www.petitpalais.paris.fr; Tue–Sun 10am–6pm, temporary exhibitions until 9pm Fri and 8pm Sat and Sun).

ARC DE TRIOMPHE

The circular area at the top of the Champs-Élysées is popularly known to Parisians as *l'Etoile* (the star), after the 12 avenues branching out from its centre. Officially renamed **place Charles de Gaulle** after the death of the president in 1970, it is dominated by one of the most familiar Paris icons, the **Arc de Triomphe** ⓴ (www.monuments-nationaux.fr; daily Oct–Mar 10am–10.30pm, Apr–Sep 10am–11pm). The arch is 50m (164ft) high and 45m (148ft) wide. A trip to the top of the staircase (lift for the disabled only) affords excellent views. It is from here that you can best appreciate the *tour de force* of geometric planning that the avenues represent.

Napoleon I conceived of the Arc de Triomphe as a tribute to his armies, and it bears the names of hundreds of his marshals and generals, and dozens of victories. No defeats are recorded, naturally, although a few of the victories are debatable. Napoleon himself only ever saw a wood-and-canvas model, since the arch was not completed until the 1830s. It rapidly became the focus for state occasions, such as the return of the emperor's remains from St Helena in 1840 and the funeral of Victor Hugo in 1885. At the Liberation, this was the spot where General de Gaulle began his triumphal march down the Champs-Élysées.

Under the arch is the grave of the Unknown Soldier. Since 1920, it has been the last resting place of a soldier who died in World War I. The eternal flame was lit here in 1923.

TROCADÉRO

Dominating place du Trocadéro is the **Palais de Chaillot** ㉑, built for the Paris World Fair of 1937. The imposing Art Deco palace was designed in the shape of an amphitheatre, with its wings following the original outline of the old Trocadéro in graceful symmetry. The west wing is home to the **Musée National de la Marine** (http://en.musee-marine. fr; closed for renovations until 2021). Also here is the Musée de l'Homme

Arc de Triomphe

(www.museedelhomme.fr). The east wing houses the **Cité de l'Architecture et du Patrimoine** (www.citedelarchitecture.fr; Wed–Mon 11am–7pm, Thu until 9pm), which combines Paris's old architecture museum with the Institut Français d'Architecture.

On avenue des Nations-Unies is **Cinéaqua** (www.cineaqua.com; daily 10am–7pm), a vast aquarium with cinema and animation studio. There are dozens of tanks containing some 9,000 fish, grouped in mini marine ecosystems.

Down avenue du Président Wilson is the vast **Palais de Tokyo ㉒**, built as the Electricity Pavilion for the 1937 World Fair. One wing was intended to hold post-1905 fine art from the municipal fine-art collection; the other wing (now the Site de Création Contemporaine) was planned for the national collection of modern art. The **Musée d'Art Moderne de la Ville de Paris** (www.mam.paris.fr; Tue–Sun 10am–6pm, Thu until 11pm during exhibitions; free but charge for temporary exhibitions. The

⊙ APP HAPPY

With the ubiquity of smart phones, it is no surprise that Paris has some very handy apps for use on the go. One of the best is the RATP public transport authority's slick, free guide to its entire network, with live traffic updates, maps and route planning capabilities. Heetch works in the same way as Uber, but solely for late-night travellers - from 8pm to 6am. Le Fooding Guide is created by Parisians and has recommendations for the best places to eat in the city. Another free guide is produced by the Louvre, and has maps of the museum and useful background on its most popular exhibits. Secrets de Paris reveals a different gem every day – from hidden streets to obscure monuments.

entrance is located on the Seine's side – 12–14 avenue de New York – until autumn 2019) opened there in 1961. In 1977 the core collection of French and international art was given a new home at the Centre Pompidou. Whereas the emphasis at the Centre Pompidou is on international art, here the focus is on artists who worked in Paris.

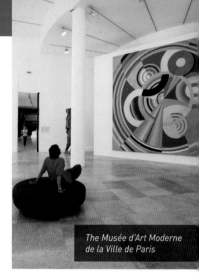

The Musée d'Art Moderne de la Ville de Paris

In the other wing is the **Site de Création Contemporaine** (www.palaisde tokyo.com; Sun–Mon noon–midnight), where a multi-disciplinary programme focuses on young artists through exhibitions, performances and workshops.

Opposite the Palais de Tokyo to the north is the Palais Musée de la Mode-Galliera de la Ville de Paris (10 avenue Pierre 1er de Serbie; www.palaisgalliera.paris.fr; closed for renovation but due to re-open in late 2019), which houses the city's collection of clothes and accessories dating from the 18th century to the present day.

WESTERN PARIS

West of the Palais de Chaillot, Passy is an upmarket, villagey residential area with a couple of busy shopping streets (rue de Passy and rue de l'Assomption). It is also home to the atmospheric **Maison de Balzac** (www.maisondebalzac.paris. fr; 47 rue Raynouard), which is under renovation but due to

Sacré-Cœur

re-open in summer 2019. Balzac penned much of his great opus *La Comédie Humaine* here.

Also in the west of Paris is the **Musée Marmottan-Monet** (www.marmottan. com, 2 rue Louis-Boilly, Sun–Mon 10am–6pm, Thu until 9pm), showcase for the art assembled by collector Louis Marmottan (1856–1932). The displays are comprised mostly of Impressionist masterpieces, including works by Monet, Renoir, Manet and Gauguin, but there is also some exceptional First Empire furniture.

BOIS DE BOULOGNE

In western Paris is the capital's biggest park, comprising 900 hectares (2,200 acres) of grassland, lakes and woods. Inspired by Hyde Park in London, Napoleon III commissioned Baron Haussmann to transform a remnant of an old hunting forest into a public park. The plans included the **Bagatelle**, once a royal retreat, which now has both manicured and English-landscape style gardens. Also within the park is a craft museum, a boating lake, the **Jardin d'Acclimatation** (www.jardindacclimatation.fr) amusement park with attractions for children, and two racecourses: Longchamp for flat races; Auteuil for steeplechases. However, parts of the park after dark are considered to be among the most dangerous places in Paris. Adjacent to the park is the $143 million futuristic building of **Fondation Louis Vuitton** (www.fondationlouisvuitton.fr) opened in 2014. Designed by the famous architect Frank Gehry, it gives shelter to a museum, exhibition spaces, bookstore and restaurant.

AROUND MONCEAU

Overlooking Parc Monceau, the **Musée Nissim de Camondo** (63 rue de Monceau; www.lesartsdecoratifs.fr; Wed–Sun 10am–5.30pm) was built by a wealthy Jewish banking family in the style of the Petit Trianon (see page 87) at Versailles. The remarkable collection of tapestries, carpets, porcelain, furniture and paintings, all dating from the 18th century, were bequeathed to the state in 1935 by the passionate art collector, Count Moïse de Camondo, in memory of his son, Nissim, killed in action in 1917. The building and family history are as fascinating as the collection.

Also beside Parc Monceau is the **Musée Cernuschi** (7 avenue Vélasquez, www.cernuschi.paris.fr; Tue–Sun 10am–6pm; permanent collections free), one of the most important collections of Oriental art in Europe. The 19th-century financier Henri Cernuschi amassed the collection on a tour of China and Japan, and built this mansion to house it.

South of Parc Monceau, at 158 boulevard Haussmann, is the **Musée Jacquemart-André ㉓** (www.musee-jacquemart-andre.com; daily 10am–6pm, until 8.30pm Mon during exhibitions). The museum displays art and furniture that once belonged to wealthy collector Edouard André and his wife, erstwhile society portrait painter Nélie Jacquemart. The house is magnificent, and its fine-art collection includes works by Bellini, Boucher, David, Donatello, Uccello, Rembrandt and Titian. The gorgeous café, decorated with chandeliers and antiques, is also worth a visit.

MONTMARTRE & PIGALLE

With narrow, winding streets and dead-ends, **Montmartre** (*'la Butte'*, or the hill, to its residents) still has something of a provincial feel. For over 200 years it has been associated with artists and bohemians. The tourist *Montmartrobus* (www.ratp.fr) spares you the walk and shows you some of the area in a single sweep, but the best way to discover Montmartre at your own pace is to start early, at the top. Take the Métro to Abbesses and the lift to the street (the stairs here seem endless) – and note the handsome Art Nouveau entrance as you leave. Rue Yvonne le Tac leads to the base station of a funicular railway.

SACRÉ-CŒUR

The funicular (Métro/bus tickets are valid) climbs to the terrace right in front of the Byzantine-style basilica of **Sacré-Cœur 24** (www.sacre-coeur-montmartre.com; basilica daily 6am–10.30pm, crypt and dome 9am–6pm; charge for crypt and dome). Standing at the highest point in Paris, it is one of the city's principal landmarks, even if some people still scorn it as a vulgar pastiche. The Sacré-Cœur's white appearance comes from the local Château-Landon limestone, which bleaches on contact with carbon dioxide in the air and hardens with age. For many, the best reason to visit the basilica is the view of the city from the dome or the terrace below.

PLACE DU TERTRE

A few steps west of Sacré-Cœur is **St-Pierre-de-Montmartre**, one of the city's oldest churches. Consecrated in 1147, it is a significant work of the early Gothic style, belied by its 18th century facade. Nearby **place du Tertre** was once the centre of village life. The square is best visited early in the morning,

Moulin Rouge – you can't miss it

before the pushy portrait artists set up their easels and the crowds of tourists take over.

On place Emile Goudeau, just downhill but artistically on an altogether much higher level, No. 13 was the site of the studio known as the **Bateau-Lavoir** (so-called because the building resembled the Seine's laundry boats until it was destroyed by fire). It was here that Picasso, Georges Braque and Juan Gris developed Cubism, Modigliani painted, and Apollinaire wrote his first Surrealist verses. Some of their predecessors – Renoir, Van Gogh and Gauguin – once lived and worked just north of place du Tertre.

The **Cimetière de Montmartre** ㉕ (daily 9am–6pm) is at 20 avenue Rachel. The cemetery's more illustrious tenants include composers Berlioz and Offenbach, the sculptor Degas, German poet Heinrich Heine and film director François Truffaut.

La Géode

PIGALLE

At the far end of rue Lepic, a market street renowned for its food shops and several appealingly bohemian cafés, is place Blanche, where the ambience changes. On the corner of boulevard de Clichy is the iconic **Moulin Rouge** (see page 98), still staging its nightly cabarets, although mostly to tourists. Next door is **La Machine du Moulin Rouge**, a huge nightclub, pumping with the sounds of house, dance music and mainstream pop. Less artistic attractions abound in **Pigalle**, a powerhouse of the Paris sex trade for decades. Tassled curtains provide glimpses of smoky interiors, garish signs promote live sex shows and pushy bouncers attempt to entice passers-by.

However, Pigalle's sleaze has been tempered by trendy nightlife venues. The cabarets that formerly occupied half the houses along rue des Martyrs are increasingly being taken over by hip clubs and fashionable bars.

LA VILLETTE

In northeast Paris, right against the Périphérique ring road, is the **Parc de la Villette** ㉖ (Métro: Porte de Pantin or Porte de la Villette, http://lavillette.com). Laid out on the site of an enormous abattoir, which was rendered obsolete by improved refrigeration techniques and poor design (the cows could not get up the steps), 55 hectares (136 acres) of futuristic gardens surround a colossal science museum, the **Cité des Sciences et de l'Industrie** (www. cite-sciences.fr; Tue–Sat 10am–6pm, Sun until 7pm).

Begin at 'L'Univers' (Universe), which has a spectacular planetarium and also provides an explanation of the Big Bang. 'La Vie' (Life) is an eclectic mix of medicine, agriculture and economics. 'La Matière' (Matter) reproduces a nuclear explosion and gives you the chance to land an Airbus 320, and 'La Communication' has displays of artificial intelligence, three-dimensional graphics and virtual reality. On the ground floor is the Cité des Enfants, which has interactive exhibits and activities for children aged 2–12 years. Outside the main entrance is L'Argonaute, a retired naval submarine.

La Géode (www.lageode.fr; Mon times vary, Tue–Sun 10.30am–6.30pm, variable hours on Mon) is a giant silver ball housing a wraparound IMAX cinema.

The former cattle market now houses a cultural and conference centre in the immense 19th century Grande Halle. Next door, the **Cité de la Musique - Philharmonie de Paris** is an edifice of angles designed by architect Christian de

⊙ ALONG THE CANAL

The Paris canals were dug in 1821 as a transport link for the factories and warehouses in the area northeast of the Bastille. Shielded by trees, the canal is a popular strolling ground, particularly on balmy summer evenings. A pleasant way to experience it is by canal boat, starting either at Bastille or at La Villette. Canal tours lasting around two and a half hours are run by Canauxrama (tel: 01 42 39 15 00; www.canauxrama.com).

Portzamparc, and includes the **Musée de la Musique** (http://philharmoniedeparis.fr; Tue–Fri noon–6pm, Sat & Sun 10am–6pm). Portzamparc also designed the national music and dance conservatory on the other side of the Grande Halle. The museum charts the development of classical, jazz and folk music and houses an impressive collection of over 4,500 musical instruments.

The impressive gardens of the park are the biggest to be built in Paris since Haussmann's time. Designed by Bernard Tschumi and opened in 1993, they comprise several thematic areas such as the Jardin des Frayeurs Enfantines (Garden of Childhood Fears) with a huge dragon slide, and the Jardin des Vents (Garden of Winds), home to multicoloured bamboo. Abstraction continues in the form of Tschumi's folies: red angular 'tree houses' (minus the trees), each with a special function such as play area, workshop, daycare centre or café.

LATIN QUARTER & ST-GERMAIN-DES-PRÉS

The area referred to as the Latin Quarter lies to the east of boulevard St-Michel. This maze of ancient streets and squares has been the stamping ground of students for nearly eight centuries and it is home to the city's most famous university, the Sorbonne. Latin was virtually the mother tongue until Napoleon put a stop to it after the Revolution. West of boulevard St-Michel is St-Germain-des-Prés, once the centre of literary Paris and existentialism, with the oldest church in Paris at its heart. Although these two areas have changed over the past few decades, with high fashion increasingly replacing heavy thinking, they still maintain their charm in tree-lined boulevards, narrow streets and beautifully manicured gardens.

THE LATIN QUARTER

Begin your visit to the Latin Quarter at **place St-Michel**, where students buy their books or gather around the grand 1860s fountain by Gabriel Davioud. From here, plunge into the narrow streets of the **St-Séverin** quarter to the east (rues St-Séverin, de la Harpe and Galande). Here, you will find medieval streets teeming with Greek restaurants, Tunisian bakeries selling sticky date pastries, and art-house cinemas.

Second-hand book stall

The early Gothic church of **St-Julien-le-Pauvre**, located on the street of the same name, hosts regular recitals of chamber and religious music. Just across rue St-Jacques stands the exquisite 13th to 15th century flamboyant Gothic church of **St-Séverin**, in which Dante is said to have prayed and French composer Camille Saint-Saëns asked to be made honorary organist.

The Sorbonne

Named after the 13th-century college established by Robert de Sorbon for poor theological students, the university was later taken in hand by Cardinal Richelieu, who financed its reconstruction (1624–42). Few of the somewhat forbidding buildings are open to the public, but you can go inside the 17th century **courtyard** with its ornate sundial and see the outside of the Baroque library and domed church.

Musée National du Moyen Age

Protests against over-crowding, antiquated teaching, bureaucracy and the basis of the social system made the Sorbonne a focal point for unrest in 1968, a year of ferment across Europe. Over on the tree-shaded **place de la Sorbonne**, it is hard to imagine the police invading such a peaceful sanctuary, one that for centuries guaranteed student immunity. But invade they did, and revolt exploded onto the streets. Students and workers made common cause, and there followed widespread national strikes that threatened the survival of the government. In the aftermath of the revolts, the Sorbonne was absorbed into the huge Paris Universities monolith and lost its independence.

Musée National du Moyen Age – Thermes de Cluny

Opposite the Sorbonne's rue des Ecoles entrance is the **Musée National du Moyen Age** ㉗ (6 place Paul-Painlevé; www.musee-moyenage.fr; Wed–Mon 9.15am–5.45pm), still often called by its former name, the Musée de Cluny. Once the residence of the Abbots of Cluny, the museum houses one of the world's finest collections of medieval artefacts. Its star attraction is the exquisite, 15th-century tapestry *La Dame à la Licorne* (The Lady and the Unicorn), six pieces depicting the five senses and the temptations that the eponymous lady vows to overcome. The museum also holds 21 of the original heads of the Kings of Judah, sculpted in 1220 for Notre-Dame cathedral, but vandalised in the Revolution.

The Hôtel de Cluny was built on the remains of a huge Gallo-Roman bath house believed to have been erected in AD 200 by the guild of *nautes* (boatmen); ships' prows are carved on the arch supports of the frigidarium (cold bath house).

Panthéon

Designed in 1755 as the church of Ste-Geneviève (patron saint of Paris), the neoclassical **Panthéon** ⓴ (www.monuments-natio naux.fr; daily Oct–Mar 10am–6pm, Apr–Sept until 6.30pm) was requisitioned during the Revolution to serve as a mausoleum. In the 19th century its status oscillated between secular and sacred, but Victor Hugo's funeral in 1885 settled the issue in favour of a secular mausoleum. The interior is sparse, its walls covered with 19th century murals by Puvis de Chavannes. The crypt is a maze of corridors lined with cells containing tombs.

Rue Mouffetard

The old streets behind the Panthéon, where the bustling **rue Mouffetard** and its offshoots meet, are like a small town within the city. The stalls of rue Mouffetard's morning market are piled with appetising produce. Here, and on tiny **place de la Contrescarpe** nearby, you will find restaurants serving a wide range of international cuisine. A little to the east, signs to **Arènes de Lutèce** point to a little park that is the site of a Roman amphitheatre, partially restored after its remains were found in the 19th century.

Great thinkers

Among those interred in the Panthéon are novelist Emile Zola, socialist Jean Jaurès, Louis Braille and Pierre and Marie Curie.

On rue St-Etienne-du-Mont is the church of **St-Etienne-du-Mont** (for opening times see www.saintetiennedumont.fr). This was the parish church of the Abbey of Ste-Geneviève and still houses a shrine to the city's patron saint. The highlight is the Renaissance rood screen (1541), the only one in Paris.

Institut du Monde Arabe

Back by the Seine, but heading east, stroll past the university complex that stands on the site of the former Halles aux Vins (wine market). Designed by architect Jean Nouvel, the nearby **Institut du Monde Arabe** ㉙ (1 rue des Fossés-St-Bernard; www.imarabe.org; Tue, Wed & Fri 10am–6pm, Thu, Sat & Sun until 7pm) was built with the help of 16 Arab nations to foster cultural links between Europe and the Islamic world. Inside, a museum traces the cultures of the Arab world with first-rate exhibits. A library of over 40,000 volumes covers all aspects of Arab culture. There are two restaurants (Le Zyriab has fine views), a literary café and a bookshop.

Jardin des Plantes

Adjacent is the **Jardin des Plantes** (www.jardindes plantes.net; daily 8am– 6.30pm, until 5pm in winter – but times change regularly depending on the season, so check their website), created by Louis

Institut du Monde Arabe

XIII as 'a royal garden of medicinal plants' and still a fine botanical and decorative garden, with exotic plants in the hot-houses. The oldest tree in Paris is located here.

The adjoining **Muséum National d'Histoire Naturelle** (www.mnhn. fr; Wed–Mon 10am–6pm) has renovated its venerable exhibits of fossils, skeletons, butterflies and mineral samples. The **Grande Galerie de l'Evolution** (36 rue Geoffroy-St-Hilaire; opening times as above), devoted to the origins of life on earth, is outstanding.

Les Deux Magots

ST-GERMAIN-DES-PRÉS

Once the heart of literary Paris, **St-Germain-des-Prés** covers an area stretching roughly from St-Sulpice to the Seine and bounded to the west by boulevard St-Germain. Its elegant streets house chic boutiques, yet it still retains a sense of animation, with crowded cafés spilling out onto the pavements. In the 1950s the area became a breeding ground for literature and philosophy. Writers such as Jean-Paul Sartre, Simone de Beauvoir and Albert Camus, gathered at **Les Deux Magots**, **Café de Flore** and other venues.

That said, the days of black polo-necks and beret-clad existentialists engaged in heated debate are over. The area has been colonised by designers and upmarket antiques dealers.

The Marché St-Germain shows just how much it has changed. After a tasteful restoration, the old market hall now contains boutiques, a swimming pool, an auditorium and a food market.

On the opposite side of the boulevard, the church of **St-Germain-des-Prés** ⑳ (www.parisinfo.com, Mon–Sat 8am–7.45pm, Sun 9am–8pm) is the oldest in Paris, parts of it dating from the 11th century.

Académie Française

The august Palais de l'Institut de France, home of the **Académie Française**, is north of the church of St-Germain, on quai de Conti by the Pont des Arts. It was designed by Louis le Vau in 1668 to harmonise with the Louvre across the river. The Institut began as a school for the sons of provincial gentry, financed by a legacy

---

⊙ NEW LEFT BANK

The 'new' Rive Gauche is the biggest urban renewal project since the mid-1850s. Newly created streets and buildings are going up in a zone of rusty factories and disused railway tracks that extend south along the river from the Gare d'Austerlitz. The area's centrepiece is the **Bibliothèque Nationale de France François Mitterrand** (www.bnf.fr; Tue–Sat 10am–8pm, Sun 1pm-7pm), opened in 1996; its 90m (300ft) high glass towers evoke open books. Nearby, at 34 quai d'Austerlitz, the concrete warehouses that once belonged to Paris's central port have been rebuilt as **Les Docks – Cité de la Mode et du Design** whose bright green riverfront facade is unmissable and houses a fashion school, the Institut Français de la Mode (www.ifm-paris.com), as well as multiple exhibition spaces, bars, clubs and restaurants.

from Cardinal Mazarin. Then, in 1805, the building was turned over to the Institut, which comprises the Académie Française, supreme arbiter of the French language founded by Cardinal Richelieu in 1635, and the Académies des Belles-Lettres, Sciences, Beaux-Arts, and Sciences Morales et Politiques.

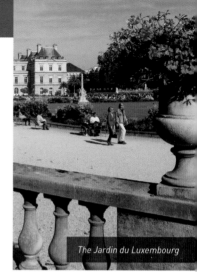
The Jardin du Luxembourg

Musée Delacroix and St-Sulpice

Tucked away in a tiny square a short walk from the church of St-Germain-des-Prés is the delightful **Musée National Eugène Delacroix** (6 place Furstenberg; www.musee-delacroix.fr; Wed–Mon 9.30am–5.30pm, until 9pm the first Thursday of every month). The painter lived here from 1857 to 1863 while he was working on frescoes in a chapel at St-Sulpice. Temporary exhibitions are held in the airy former studio, and letters and personal effects are displayed in the house. There is a wonderfully calm garden out the back.

A short hop south across boulevard St-Germain-des-Prés is place St-Sulpice, the eastern side of which is dominated by Jean-Baptiste Servandoni's Italianesque church of the same name. **St-Sulpice** (daily 7.30am–7.30pm, guided tours every Sun at 2.30pm) is notable for its vast towers, one of which is higher than the other, and for Delacroix's massive oil-and-wax frescoes, completed only two years before his death.

Jardin du Luxembourg

The beautifully landscaped **Jardin du Luxembourg** ㉜ is the quintessential Paris park. Students read, relax or play tennis, old men meet under the chestnut trees to play chess or a game of *boules*, lovers huddle together on metal chairs, and children sail boats across the carp-filled pond and ride a merry-go-round designed by Charles Garnier, architect of the historic opera house (see page 44). At the northern end of the gardens, the Italianate **Palais du Luxembourg** (guided tours one Saturday each month; tel: 01 44 54 19 30; www.senat.fr), built for Marie de Médicis in the early 17th century, now houses the French Senate. The adjacent Petit Luxembourg is the official home of the president of the Senate.

The **Musée du Luxembourg** (19 rue de Vaugirard; www.museeduluxembourg.fr; daily 10.30am–7pm, Fri until 10pm) hosts art exhibitions.

ODÉON

The Odéon district lies between the Latin Quarter and St-Germain-des-Prés. Across boulevard St-Germain, at the Carrefour de l'Odéon, a statue of the Revolutionary leader Georges Danton marks the spot where his house once stood. Fellow Revolutionary Camille Desmoulins lived at No. 2 before storming the Bastille in 1789. Others plotted to the north in neighbouring streets that now shelter some of the most expensive boutiques and apartments in Paris.

From here, rue de l'Odéon, the first street in Paris to have gutters and pavements, leads to place de l'Odéon. The neo-classical **Odéon Théâtre de l'Europe** (tel: 01 44 85 40 40; www.theatre-odeon.eu; show times vary), founded in 1782, is home to one of France's leading state theatre companies. It puts on a repertoire of mainly foreign playwrights (Büchner, Chekhov, Shakespeare, etc), sometimes in original-language productions.

AROUND THE EIFFEL TOWER

When the Paris nobility moved out of the Marais in the 18th century, and Versailles dwindled, the rich and famous built new town houses across the river from the Tuileries, in the 7th *arrondissement*. Not only is this chic district rich with upmarket architecture, it also has a wealth of visitor attractions, with highlights including the Musée d'Orsay, the Eiffel Tower, the Invalides and the Musée Rodin.

MUSÉE D'ORSAY

'The station is superb and truly looks like a Fine Arts Museum, and since the Fine Arts Museum resembles a station, I suggest... we make the change while we still can,' said painter Edouard Detaille in 1900. In 1986, his joke became a reality. Linked to the Tuileries by the Passerelle

Léopold-Sédar-Senghor footbridge, the converted 19th century hotel-cum-railway station was transformed into the **Musée d'Orsay** ❸ (www.musee-orsay.fr; Tue–Sun 9.30am–6pm, Thu until 9.45pm), devoted to French art from 1848 to 1914. Keeping the exterior much as it was, Italian architect Gae Aulenti adapted the interior to house many of the previously scattered works of that period, including the superb Impressionist collection formerly held in the Jeu de Paume (see page 42). Sculpture is well represented, and photography is covered from its inception (1839) onwards.

Many visitors start at the top with the Impressionists who include: Renoir, Cézanne, Manet and Monet before heading down to the mezzanine for the Post Impressionists, notably Van Gogh and Gauguin. Among the ground-floor collections, the vast canvases of Gustave Courbet are outstanding. Rest weary feet at Café Campana, high up behind the huge old station clock, or the beautifully-restored Restaurant du Musée d'Orsay on the second floor.

ASSEMBLÉE NATIONALE

Geographically if not temperamentally part of the Left Bank, the **Palais Bourbon** is the seat of the **Assemblée Nationale** (126 rue de l'Université) the Lower House of the French Parliament. Built from 1722 to 1728 for Louis XIV's daughter the Duchess of Bourbon, it forms a fittingly stately riverside facade for the grand 7th *arrondissement*. Built in the style of the Grand Trianon at Versailles, Napoleon later added the Grecian columns facing the Pont de la Concorde. The palace is more graceful when seen from its entrance on the south side. Only French citizens can go in, apart from on the annual Journées du Patrimoine open days, when thousands queue to see the Delacroix paintings in the library.

MUSÉE RODIN

The Prime Minister's residence, Hôtel Matignon (57 rue de Varenne), is a short walk from the Assemblée Nationale. Its private park has a music pavilion favoured for secret strategy sessions. On the same elegant street, at No. 77, Rodin's former mansion, the delightful 18th-century Hôtel Biron, is now a show-case for the sculptor's works in the form of the **Musée Rodin** ③④ (www.musee-rodin.fr; Tue–Sun 10am–5.45pm). Many of the most famous sculptures are in the gardens (Oct–Mar closure at 5pm). Highlights include *The Kiss* (removed from the Chicago World Fair of 1893 for being too shocking), *The Thinker* (reputedly Dante con-templating the Inferno), *The Burghers of Calais and Balzac,* depict-ing the writer as a mountain of a man. Also on display are works by Camille Claudel, the most famous of Rodin's mistresses.

LES INVALIDES

One of the most impor-tant sights in this area is the monumental **Hôtel des Invalides** ③⑤ (www. invalides.org; daily 10am–6pm, until 5pm in winter), established by Louis XIV as the first national hos-pital and retirement home for soldiers wounded in action. At one time it housed some 6,000 veterans, but Napoleon Bonaparte com-mandeered a large part of the building for the superb **Musée de l'Armée** (opening

Napoleon's tomb inside the Église du Dôme

times as above), a vast collection of weapons and military para-phernalia dating from medieval times to the modern era. It is, in effect, several museums in one: there are large sections devoted to the two world wars, as well as intricate 18th century models of French towns and fortresses, suits of armour, and uniforms.

The Invalides came to symbolise the glory of Napoleon him-self, when his remains were brought back from St Helena in 1840 for burial in the chapel under the golden **Eglise du Dôme** (opening times as above, July–Aug until 7pm). The emperor's son, who died of tuberculosis in Vienna, is buried in the crypt; his remains were sent here by Hitler in 1940.

The main courtyard allows access to the adjoining church of **St-Louis-des-Invalides**, decorated with flags taken by French armies in battle. The courtyard itself contains the 18 cannons, including eight taken from Vienna, which Napoleon ordered to be fired on great occasions, including the birth of his son in 1811. The cannons sounded again for the 1918 Armistice and the funeral of Marshal Foch in 1929.

Southwest of the Invalides is the **Ecole Militaire**, where officers have trained since the middle of the 18th century. Their former parade ground, the vast **Champ de Mars**, is now a green park stretching all the way to the Eiffel Tower.

THE EIFFEL TOWER

For many, the ultimate Paris monument is still the **Tour Eiffel** ③, or Eiffel Tower (www.tour-eiffel.fr; daily 9.30am–11.45pm, until midnight Jul–Aug). When Gustave Eiffel's icon was chosen as the centrepiece of the World Fair of 1889, he claimed enthusiastically, 'France will be the only country with a 300m flagpole!' But his designs were met with strong oppo-sition. The architect of the opera house, Charles Garnier, and the novelist Guy de Maupassant were its most vocal opponents;

Maupassant organised a protest picnic underneath it – 'the only place out of sight of the wretched construction'.

However, the Paris public loved their new tower, and only a few years later writers and artists such as Apollinaire, Jean Cocteau, Raoul Dufy and Maurice Utrillo heaped praise upon it. At 321m (1,054ft) the tower was the world's tallest building until 1931, when New York's Empire State Building went up. Surviving a proposal for its demolition in 1909, when the placing of a radio transmitter at the top gave it a valuable practical function, the tower is climbed by some 7 million visitors a year.

There are 360 steps to the first floor, where there are audio-visual presentations on the tower's history, a vertigo-inducing glass floor 57m (187ft) from the ground and restaurants, shops and the CinEiffel 'immersion show' in the Ferrié Pavilion. There are another 700 steps to the second floor (both first and second floors accessible by lifts, although queues are likely), which has the Michelin-starred Jules Verne restaurant (re-opening in spring 2019 after a refurbishment), shops and even a macaroon bar. At the very top of the tower, (accessible by lift only) is a glassed-in viewing platform and open-air section, a champagne bar and Gustave Eiffel's office. On a clear day panoramas of over 65km (40 miles) can be enjoyed (see page 115). On hot days the ironwork expands, enabling the tower to grow as much as 15cm (6in). Even in the strongest of winds, it has never swayed more than 12cm (4in). Up to 40 tonnes of paint have to be used when it is painted every seven years.

MUSÉE DU QUAI BRANLY

Just northeast of the tower, at 37 quai Branly, is Jacques Chirac's cultural legacy, the **Musée du Quai Branly** ❸ (www.quaibranly.fr; museum Tue, Wed & Sun 11am–7pm, Thu–Sat 11am–9pm, garden Tue, Wed & Sun 9.15am–7.30pm, Thu–Sat 9.15am–9.15pm). The museum houses a collection of around 300,000 objects of art from Africa, Asia, the Americas and Oceania, with over 3,600 items actually on display. With its colonial overtones, the collection has sparked some controversy, but the building itself – a striking foliage-covered scarlet edifice designed by Jean Nouvel – has been more warmly received.

MONTPARNASSE

Named after the mountain home of the classical Muses, 'Mount Parnassus' was a mound left after quarrying. In the 1920s, the quarter took over from Montmartre as the stamping ground of the city's artistic colony, led by Picasso. American expatriates such as Ernest Hemingway, Gertrude Stein, F. Scott Fitzgerald and John Dos Passos liked the free-living atmosphere and added to the mystique themselves.

One of Henry Miller's hangouts, Le Select (99 boulevard du Montparnasse) opened as an all-night bar in 1925. *Les Six*, the group of composers that included Milhaud, Poulenc and Honegger, met here. La Coupole (see page 115), just opposite, at No. 102, was a favourite with literary couple Sartre and de Beauvoir in the years following World War II. Le Dôme at No. 108 has lost some of its character since

A colourful mural in Montparnasse

the days of Modigliani and Stravinsky, with elaborate remodelling. Across the street, at No. 105, La Rotonde was where Picasso, Derain and Vlaminck used to meet. At the junction of boulevard du Montparnasse and boulevard St-Michel, La Closerie des Lilas is where Lenin and Trotsky dreamt of a Russian Revolution, and where Hemingway and his friends met after World War I.

Today the attraction isn't immediately evident: boulevard du Montparnasse is plain by Paris standards, and most of the haunts where the 'Lost Generation' found itself have been polished and painted, or even entirely rebuilt. But people still pay elevated prices for the privilege of sitting in a seat that may have been warmed by Modigliani, Lenin or Sartre.

The 59-storey, 210m (689ft) **Tour Montparnasse** (33 avenue du Maine; www.tuurmontparnasse56.com; Sun–Thu 9.30am–10.30pm, Fri–Sat 9.30am–11pm last entry 30 minutes before closing) may be something of an egregious eyesore, but the view

The catacombs

Beneath Montparnasse are the city's catacombs (1, avenue du Colonel Henri Rol-Tanguy - entrance on place Denfert-Rochereau; www.catacombes.paris. fr; Tue–Sun 10am–8.30pm, last admission 7.30pm), old quarries whose corridors were used for the reburial of millions of skeletons from overcrowded cemeteries and charnel houses. Unidentified, the bones are stacked on shelves or artfully arranged into macabre patterns.

from the top is marvellous. Gourmets should visit Le Ciel de Paris, which claims to be the highest panoramic restaurant in Paris.

The **Cimetière du Montparnasse** ❸ (entrance on boulevard Edgar Quinet, daily from 8–9am to 5.30–6pm depending on season) contains the tombs of composers Saint-Saëns and César Franck, writer Maupassant and poet Baudelaire, plus Alfred Dreyfus, the Jewish army officer whose conviction on trumped-up spying charges split the nation. Also buried here are car-maker André Citroën, Vichy Prime Minister Pierre Laval (executed while dying from a suicide attempt), philosopher Jean-Paul Sartre and writer Simone de Beauvoir.

LA DÉFENSE

Follow the long avenue de la Grande-Armée down from the Arc de Triomphe, and the battery of towers looms larger and larger beyond the elegant, leafy suburb of Neuilly. Cross the river and you are in a mini-Manhattan that has grown since 1969 to become a mini-city in its own right.

The **Grande Arche** ❸ is further away than most of the towers, and only when you get close do you realise how big it is. A hollow cube 110m (360ft) high and 106m (347ft) wide, it could straddle the Champs-Élysées and tuck Notre-Dame underneath it. Built with remarkable speed (Danish architect Johann-Otto von Sprekelsen won the contest in 1983 and the arch was completed in time for the bicentennial of the French Revolution in 1989), the Grande Arche stands in line with the Arc de Triomphe and the Louvre. Its white gables are clad in Carrara marble, the outer facades in a combination of grey marble and glass. The two 'legs' contain offices, and the roof houses conference rooms and exhibition spaces. Increasing numbers of visitors and office workers have given rise to a growing number of shops, cinemas, hotels and restaurants at La Défense. Most are concentrated in the **Quatre Temps** shopping centre (www.les4temps.com), which also includes

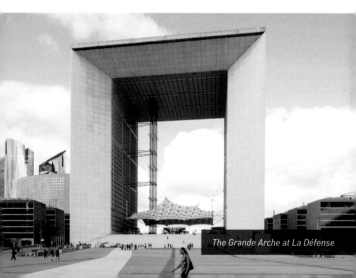

The Grande Arche at La Défense

the 16-screen UGC Ciné Cité La Défense cinema complex (www.ugc.fr).

Across the main concourse, a 12m (39ft) bronze thumb by César literally sticks out like a sore thumb. Stroll down the tiers of terraces and you will discover even more statues, fountains and murals by Miró, Calder and other modern artists, all detailed on street-plans from the Espace Défense (15 place de la Défense; www.ladefense.fr). Here you can also find out about the history of the area and the plans for Norman Foster's Heritage Plaza, due to complete in 2022.

EXCURSIONS

VERSAILLES

Louis XIV's palace at **Versailles** ⓴ is as extravagant as the Sun King was himself. A visit to the château takes most or all of a day and entails a lot of walking. Versailles is 24km (15 miles) southwest of Paris, by road (N10), by train from Gare St-Lazare to Versailles-Rive Droite, or by RER (line C) to Versailles-Rive Gauche. Opening times are Tue–Sun Apr–Oct 9am–6.30pm, Nov–Mar until 5.30pm; other parts of the estate have separate opening times. Various ticket combinations are available on the website: www.chateau versailles.fr.

Highlights of the interior include: the baroque **Royal Chapel**; the **State Apartments**, in which Louis XIV entertained; the Salon de Diane, where he played billiards; the 73m (240ft) long **Galerie des Glaces** (Hall of Mirrors); and the King's Bedroom, where Louis died of gangrene in 1715. In the Queen's Bedroom, 19 royal children were born, the births often attended by members of the court, as was the custom.

The grandest facade faces west to the gardens, where the fountains spout to music at weekends (Apr–Oct). The **Grand Trianon**, the small palace Louis XIV used when he wanted to escape the vast château; the **Petit Trianon**, favoured by Louis XV and the **Hameau** and miniature farm are also worth a visit. The Hameau was built as a place of lesiure in a vernacular, rustic style by Louis XVI's queen, Marie-Antoinette, as was the fashion among the French aristocracy of the time. It provided a more intimate setting and an escape from some of the formality of court life.

The Galerie des Glaces at Versailles

FONTAINEBLEAU

The seat of sovereigns from Louis IX to Napoleon III and a glittering example of French Mannerism, the château at **Fontainebleau** ❹ (www.musee-chateau-fontainebleau.fr; Oct–Mar Wed–Mon 9.30am–5pm, Apr–Sept until 6pm, last admission 45 mins before closing) makes a pleasant day trip from Paris. Here Louis XIV signed the Revocation of the Edict of Nantes in 1685, and Napoleon I signed his first act of abdication in 1814. More recently (1945–65) Fontainebleau was the headquarters of the military branch of NATO. Fontainebleau is 64km (40 miles) southeast of Paris by the A6 or by train from Gare de Lyon, then Ligne A bus to the château.

Châteaux day trips

Cityrama ParisVision (www.pariscityvision.com) runs day trips from Paris to Fontainebleau and Vaux-le-Vicomte as well as guided tours and candlelit visits.

MALMAISON

Set in lovely grounds, the château at **Malmaison** 42 (http://en.musees-nation aux-malmaison.fr; Wed–Mon Apr–Sept 10am–12.30pm, 1.30–5.45pm, Sat–Sun until 6.15pm, Oct–Mar 10am–12.30pm and 1.30–5.15pm, Sat–Sun until 5.45pm) was the home of Napoleon's wife, Josephine, who continued to live here after their divorce. Many of her possessions are on display. Malmaison is 6km (4 miles) west of Paris. Métro: Grande Arche de La Défense, then bus 258, or RER to Rueil-Malmaison, followed by bus Optile 27.

VAUX-LE-VICOMTE

This 17th-century château (www.vaux-le-vicomte.com; mid-Mar–mid-Nov daily 10am–5.15pm, candlelit visits May–mid-Oct Sat 8pm–midnight) was designed by Louis Le Vau, André Le Nôtre and Charles Le Brun for Louis XIV's finance minister, Fouquet. No sooner was it completed than the king had its owner arrested for embezzlement and jailed for life. **Vaux-le-Vicomte** 43 is 55km (35 miles) southeast of Paris on the N5 or by train from Gare de Lyon to Melun, then a taxi ride.

GIVERNY

Claude Monet lived at this house in **Giverny** 44 (www.fondation-monet.com; Apr–Oct daily 9.30am–6pm, last admission 5.30pm) from 1883 to 1926 and painted the gardens many times, especially the water lilies (see the Musée de l'Orangerie, page 42). Giverny is situated 85km (53 miles) northwest of Paris by the A13, D181 and D5, or by train from Gare St-Lazare to Vernon, with a shuttle bus from the station to Giverny.

DISNEYLAND PARIS

Disneyland Paris ⑮ (www.disneylandparis.com; daily, times vary but usually 10am–8pm, Studios Park usually 10am–6pm, extra 'Magic Time' 8.30am–9.30pm, check website for any temporary closures) is an ambitious recreation complex that encompasses a theme park, hotels, restaurants, a convention cen-

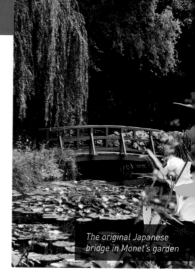

The original Japanese bridge in Monet's garden

tre, a golf course, tennis courts and swimming pools; and attracts over 16 million visitors a year. In the theme park itself, Main Street USA recaptures the traditions of small-town America at the turn of the 20th century, and leads to four other 'lands' – Frontierland, Adventureland, Fantasyland and Discoveryland. Each themed section has a variety of fun experiences to offer. Every day at 7pm there is a parade including floats inspired by the famous Disney movies. In the **Walt Disney Studios Park** visitors can explore film sets; the Twilight Zone Tower of Terror thrill ride ends with a sheer drop into a black hole. It is worth using the Fastpass scheme (free, available at ride ticket machines) to beat the queues.

The resort is 32km (20 miles) east of Paris, near Marne-la-Vallée. A motorway gives access from the city and the airports, Charles-de-Gaulle and Orly. Speedy commuter trains (RER line A) from the capital and even faster long-distance trains (TGV) serve Marne-la-Vallée/Chessy station near the entrance.

Items for sale at the Marché de St-Ouen

WHAT TO DO

Critics of Paris sometimes dismiss it as a 'museum city', a conglomeration too reverently preserved in aspic. Nothing could be further from the truth. The past matters, but this is also one of the liveliest and most influential cultural powerhouses in the world, with an enormous army of contemporary creators and outlets for film, theatre, music and fashion. It's also a consumer paradise, with some of the best shops you'll find anywhere.

SHOPPING

The range of shops in Paris is vast. There are the eye-poppingly expensive jewellers on elegant place Vendôme, the high fashion icons in formerly literary St-Germain-des-Prés, the much-loved book stalls on the banks of the Seine, and the ever-popular flea markets on the edges of the city. There's also an enduring tradition of small, specialist retailers.

WHAT TO BUY WHERE

Each neighbourhood has its own mood and atmosphere, and the shops often reflect its history and the people who live there. In terms of fashion, expect boho designers in Montmartre; designer couture on rue du Faubourg-St-Honoré and avenue Montaigne; and cool, contemporary streetwear

Gourmet paradise

Paris is a famously foodie city, and every *quartier* has its *chocolatiers*, superb *pâtisseries* and *boulangeries* (bakers), *boucheries* (butchers), delicatessens, ripe-smelling *fromageries* (cheese shops) and bustling street markets.

around rue Etienne-Marcel. The exclusive 7th *arrondissement* is good for traditional menswear, along with upmarket interior design boutiques. Chic place Vendôme glitters with diamond-encrusted baubles, but you will find more original pieces in St-Germain-des-Prés or the Marais. Opulent antiques are sold around quai Voltaire in the 7th and rue du Faubourg-St-Honoré in the 8th. Retro furnishing and ceramics from the 1960s and '70s are popular near Bastille and Montmartre.

That said, the shopping map of Paris is far from static, reflecting an ebb and flow that goes with the rise and fall of different areas. The Champs-Élysées, which zigzagged from the epitome of glamour in the early 20th century to that of tourist dross in the 1980s, started returning to favour in the 1990s, and is now buzzing with upmarket brands including multi-brand store LE66 (www.le66.fr). Historically-staid rue St-Honoré is now the focus for a more avant-garde fashion set and, similarly, designer fashion has migrated to once-literary St-Germain-des-Prés.

Since the 1990s, restoration of its beautiful *hôtels particuliers* and the installation of several important museums have transformed the Marais into a highly international district with youthful fashion boutiques and cutting-edge design shops. Rue Charlot, in the 3rd, is a hive of contemporary fashion activity, while the hub of the Marais' fashionable area around rue Vieille-du-Temple has a wealth of independent bookshops and clothing stores.

Some neighbourhoods reflect the changing population of Paris. In the 13th *arrondissement,* with its large South-East Asian population, you'll find Chinese supermarkets and *pâtisseries* among the high-rise tower blocks. Another overlooked corner over in the 10th, the Canal St-Martin has resolutely made its mark on the retail map, highlighted by the three colourful shops of quirky fashion retailer Antoine et Lili.

Other areas have not fared as well: the aristocratic history of the boulevards of Bonne Nouvelle and Montmartre is now a distant memory smudged by discount stores and fast-food chains. Forum des Halles, right in the heart of the city, used to be the epitome of retail decline, with its three-level underground shopping mall long reviled for its array of brash chain stores, but after a huge

Ultra-trendy Merci concept store in the Marais

regeneration project, the ugly 1970s Forum building has been replaced by a gleaming new cultural and shopping complex, together with a pretty park, which is partially sheltered by a massive green glass canopy. It currently boasts 127 stores, including exclusive brands such as L'Exception and Celio, together with 22 restaurants, a cinema, a gym, an Olympic-sized swimming pool, a media library and a hip-hop centre.

MARKETS

The city's markets pull in bargain hunters, foodies and collectors alike. There are three main flea markets: in the 18th *arrondissement*, the famous Marché aux Puces de St-Ouen, which is the largest of its kind in the world, the smaller Marché aux Puces de la Porte de Vanves, and, in the 12th *arrondissement*, the Marché d'Aligre. Slightly down-scale, but every bit as popular, is the Puces de Montreuil market in the 20th

The daily market on rue Mouffetard

arrondissement. Roving street markets (Marché Volant) are held two or three mornings a week (usually in the morning); at these you can find authentic produce and a distinctive local character.

In addition there are over 50 street markets; some have just a few stalls, whereas others, such as Marché Bastille or Marché de l'avenue Daumesnil, stretch for hundreds of metres and have a superb range of stock. Market streets, including rue Mouffetard, in the Latin Quarter, have food shops with stalls that spill onto the pavement and are open all day from Tuesday to Saturday, with a long break for lunch, and on Sunday morning. For a full list with opening times, see http://meslieux.paris.fr/marches.

SPORTS

The city caters fairly well for the sports enthusiast. You can find details on sporting events in the Wednesday edition of *Le*

Figaro. For comprehensive information about sporting facilities visit www.parisinfo.com.

SPECTATOR SPORTS

Football and rugby fans can watch games at the huge **Stade de France** (rue Francis de Pressensé, St-Denis; www.stadefrance.com) just north of the city ringroad. The **Parc des Princes** (22 rue du Commandant Guilbaud; www.psg.fr) is home to Paris's premier division football team, Paris St-Germain. The huge **AccorHotels Arena** (8 boulevard de Bercy; www.accorhotelsarena.com), and now hosts events such as ice skating, motor sports, basketball, handball and tennis**. It can hold up to 20,300 spectators**.

For horse racing, the Grand Prix de l'Arc de Triomphe takes place in October, at **Longchamp** in the Bois de Boulogne.

PARTICIPANT SPORTS

The few public tennis courts in Paris, such as those at the Jardin du Luxembourg, are available on a first-come-first-served basis. Municipal swimming pools include the **Piscine Josephine Baker**, which floats on the Seine and has a retractable roof for warm weather. For details of municipal sports facilities, see www.parisinfo.com. The quais de Seine, Bois de Boulogne and Canal St-Martin offer good cycling opportunities; the **Fédération Française de Cyclotourisme**, http://ffvelo.fr, has details of cycling clubs.

Sporting events

Major sporting events include the Six Nations Cup in Feb/March, the Marathon in April, and the French Tennis Open in May/June at the Stade Roland-Garros.

ENTERTAINMENT

For event listings, check *Pariscope* (www.pariscope.fr) or *L'Officiel des Spectacles* (www.offi.fr). The Wednesday supplement of *Le Figaro* is another good source. Up-to-date information can also be found at www.parisinfo.com.

THEATRE

The main national theatre is the **Comédie Française** (1 place Colette; www.comedie-francaise.fr), where works by such revered writers as Molière and Racine are performed. Modern classics are shown here and at the **Théâtre du Vieux Colombier** (21 rue du Vieux-Colombier; www.theatreduvieux colombier.com); the **Théâtre du Châtelet** (2 rue Edouard Colonne, www.chatelet-theatre.com) hosts opera, classical concerts and the occasional ballet.

⊙ CINEMA

Paris has many multi-screen cinemas showing the latest blockbusters, but if you would rather see a French classic, there are dozens of good art-house cinemas too. Most cinemas in the centre of Paris show films in their original language with sub-titles in French ('VO' – *version originale*). One of the most unique cinemas in Europe, the exotic **La Pagode**, closed its doors in 2015, but it is slated to be restored and re-opened in the next three years. In the meantime, cinema buffs can also pay homage at the **Cinémathèque Française** (51 rue de Bercy, www.cinematheque.fr) which is located in a Cubist-inspired building by Frank Gehry.

OPERA AND BALLET

Opera and ballet are staged in the lavish **Palais Garnier** (place de l'Opéra) and in the modern **Opéra Bastille** (place de la Bastille) www.operadeparis.fr.

JAZZ, POP AND ROCK

Paris has excellent jazz credentials and a long list of clubs. An established venue is the **Caveau de la Huchette** (5 rue de la Huchette; www.caveaudelahuchette.fr). **Le Sunset/**

Cinémathèque Française

Sunside (60 rue des Lombards; www.sunset-sunside.com) is two jazz clubs in one: electric jazz and world music, plus acoustic. Bigger names perform at **New Morning** (7 & 9 rue des Petites-Ecuries; www.newmorning.com) and the **Jazz Club Etoile** (Le Méridien; 81 boulevard Gouvion-St-Cyr; www.jazzclub-paris.com).

Pop and rock concerts are held at the **Zénith** in the Parc de la Villette (see page 66), the **Stade de France**, Parc des Princes, and the **AccorHotels Arena** (see page 95). Ticket offices (*billeteries*) at branches of the Fnac chain (www.fnac.com) will have details of who is playing.

CABARETS

Lavish nearly-nude cabarets, geared mainly for tourists, hark back to the capital's 'naughty' image of yesteryear. The **Lido** (116 bis av. des Champs-Élysées; www.lido.fr) and the **Folies Bergère** (32 rue Richer; www.foliesbergere.com) are classic survivors. **Crazy Horse** (12 av. George V; www.lecrazy horseparis.com) puts on slick yet knowingly tongue-in-cheek shows. The celebrated **Moulin Rouge** (82 blvd de Clichy; www. moulinrouge.fr) puts on two shows a night.

CLUBS AND BARS

The words 'Paris nightlife' make many visitors think of Montmartre and Montparnasse, but these days the biggest after-dark buzz is around rue Oberkampf in the east of the city. **Café Charbon** (109 rue Oberkampf; www.nouveaucasino.net) launched the area's nightlife boom two decades ago and is still going strong; behind it is the same management's **Nouveau Casino** one of the liveliest nightclubs in the city. Nearby **L'Alimentation Générale** (64 rue Jean-Pierre Timbaud; www.alimentation-generale.net) is a cavernous bar with club nights and world music concerts.

Exciting venues are not confined to the east. **Showcase** (Pont Alexandre III; www.showcase.fr) is a club underneath the Right Bank end of the Pont Alexandre III, which attracts a trendy young crowd.

In the centre of town, film director David Lynch set up the city's first members' bar, the very swanky and atmospheric **Club Silencio** (142 rue Montmartre; www.silencio-club.com); non-members can get in after 11pm. Another big-name central drinking den is **Harry's Bar** (5 rue Daunou). Hemingway, Gershwin and others frequented this authentic Paris institution. The cocktails are excellent – and strong.

Further north, and with a more youthful, electro vibe, is **Point Ephémère** (200 quai de Valmy; www.pointephemere.org), set on the bank of the Canal St-Martin a short walk southwest from Jaurès Métro station. This clubbing and concert venue also has a good restaurant and café, a waterfront terrace in summer, and a gallery.

The Marais is arguably the hippest neighbourhood in Paris, where fashion, art and the gay scene mix, with institutions like Raidd (23 rue du Temple) and hip hideaways such as **Little Red Door** (60 rue Charlot; www.lrdparis.com).

For information about clubs and concerts, pick up the free, fortnightly pocket magazine *Lylo* (www.lylo.fr) in trendy bars and music shops.

Showcase - Parisian club

CHILDREN

For most children, Disneyland (www.disneylandparis.com) (see page 89) will be far more appealing than any city sightseeing. For a cheaper alternative, an afternoon in one of Paris's parks (see pages 41 and 76) might do the trick. For small children there are merry-go-rounds, puppet theatres (not Jul–Aug), pony rides and toy boats in the **Jardin du Luxembourg**. The **Jardin d'Acclimatation** (see page 62) is a children's park with a zoo, pony rides and puppet shows in the Bois de Boulogne. For the scientifically minded, there is a lot to learn in the **Cité des Sciences et de l'Industrie** (see page 67), where the Cité des Enfants is aimed at children aged 2–12. Kids can also get hands on with science at the **Palais de la Découverte** (see page 58) on the Champs-Élysées.

CALENDAR OF EVENTS

For details of these and other events, see www.parisinfo.com.

January Chinese New Year, Chinatown. Métro: Porte d'Ivry.

Spring Foire du Trône (late March–early May), a monster funfair at Pelouse de Reuilly, Bois de Vincennes, Métro: Porte Dorée.

April Paris Marathon ends on the Champs-Élysées.

Good Friday The Archbishop of Paris leads Procession of the Cross up the steps of Sacré-Cœur basilica, Montmartre, Métro: Anvers.

May/June French Open Tennis Championships, chic Grand Slam event, Roland-Garros stadium, Métro: Porte d'Auteuil.

June For the Fête de la Musique (Music Festival) on the 21st, there are free concerts all over Paris.

July Bastille Day (14th). Festivities include a military parade along the Champs-Élysées, a firework display at the Trocadéro and dancing on place de la Bastille. The Tour de France ends on the Champs-Élysées. Paris Cinéma, international film festival, screenings at various venues. Night-time firework displays and illuminated fountains at the Château de Versailles (mid-July–mid-Sept).

July/August Paris-Plages, the wildly successful 'city beach' brings sand, palm trees and a host of open-air attractions and entertainment to the banks of river and canal for four weeks. See www.paris.fr.

September Journées du Patrimoine, open days at otherwise off-limits government and private buildings.

October Prix de l'Arc de Triomphe, France's biggest horse race, Longchamp, Bois de Boulogne, Métro: Porte d'Auteuil and free shuttle-bus. Festival d'Automne, the annual festival of theatre, music and dance (until December). Nuit Blanche, museums and cultural venues open late on the first Saturday of the month, with special events laid on. See www.paris.fr.

November The arrival of Beaujolais Nouveau (third Tuesday of the month) is celebrated in bars and restaurants.

December Christmas markets, La Défense and Champs-Élysées. Notre-Dame is packed for 11pm Christmas Eve Mass. New Year's Eve crowds pour onto the Champs-Élysées, and there are fireworks at the Trocadéro.

EATING OUT

Paris is considered one of the culinary capitals of the world, and deservedly so. In the 2000s, the French capital's dining scene was criticised for being slow to evolve, unlike other competitors on the international stage. Such concerns have been more or less neutralised by the steady rise of regional and international cuisines, the runaway success of a number of young owner-chefs, often working in tiny or canteen-style premises, and by the local 'fooding' trend and global slow food movement.

The downside is that eating out in Paris is more expensive than ever, and good bargain bistro fare – the sort of thing visitors to Paris used to rave about on their return home – is harder to find. Consult the list of recommendations in this guide (see page 108) and get the lowdown on the latest new openings in the free weekly guide *A Nous Paris* (www.anousparis.fr), available on Mondays in Métro stations. Websites Le Fooding (www.lefooding.com) and Paris By Mouth (www.parisbymouth.com) and app The Fork are all worth checking out for local recommendations.

Chez Prune, great for tapas and people-watching

The Louvre's elegant Café Marly

CLASSIC TO CONTEMPORARY

The great cuisines of the world can be counted on one hand, and French cuisine is one of them. What the term implies is an established, coherent body of ingredients, techniques and dishes, which have all been developed, studied and perfected by masters of the art over many years.

This is not to say that French food isn't evolving. New flavours are integrated into the cooking all the time, albeit carefully. Curry, lime, peppers, coconut and lemongrass are all fairly common ingredients on gastronomic menus. Most dishes remain French at the core, but exotic nuances are certainly part of the high-end experience. In the middle ground, couscous is eaten almost as often as *bœuf bourguignon*, and sushi seems to be the city's favourite fast food.

Even in terms of technique, French cooking has modernised; sauces and pastries, for example, tend to be lighter than they were previously, and vegetables are more prevalent. Menus have been simplified and better aligned to contemporary appetites.

The advantage of this from a visitor's perspective is that the classic dishes we dream about can still be found in authentic form on French tables. If you want French onion soup, you can find it. If you order *steak au poivre*, out will come that desired slab of beef in a creamy, peppery sauce that spills across the plate towards your crispy pile of *frites*.

Another thing that makes French food extraordinary (and the bad French food, on a gracious day, forgivable) is the degree to which it is social. Even with the increased pace of modern life, the French still believe in sitting down and sharing meals in good company over a bottle of wine – so much so, indeed, that one of the most prominent fashions in recent years has been for canteen-style restaurants where diners rub up together on plain wooden benches seated at long communal tables. After all, food in France is much more than just sustenance.

⊘ LE FOODING

The term 'Le Fooding', coined in 1999 by journalist Alexandre Cammas, joins the two English words 'food' and 'feeling' to express an attitude towards dining that emphasises emotion, atmosphere, alluring food presentation, imagination, entertainment and time, as much as high-quality food on the plate. Says Cammas, 'People need a lot more than just good food to feel well fed.' It's all about approaching the table with the mind and all the senses, not just an empty belly and a greedy tongue. In a way, this is what France has always been famous for. For restaurants that share these ideals, visit www.lefooding.com.

WHERE TO EAT

Bistros tend to serve simple, traditional dishes. The food quality varies from one to the next, unlike the menus, which are practically carbon copies of one another: potato and herring salad, duck confit, beef daube, chocolate mousse and tarte Tatin are a few of the classic dishes. Brasseries (the louder, brighter, Belle Epoque option) often offer similar fare, but also specialise in seafood – heaps of oysters, mussels, langoustines, lobsters and clams spinning past on waiters' dexterous palms – and Alsatian dishes such as choucroute.

Standard, everyday cafés usually serve sandwiches, notably the classic *croque-monsieur* (grilled ham and cheese) and a variety of salads. However, modern cafés – trendy, chic establishments that pack in fashionable crowds – serve full menus, typically of contemporary, cosmopolitan food with a Mediterranean bent, and often at prices to match full-blown restaurants.

Tipping

A service charge of 12 to 15 percent is, by law, included in the price given at restaurants, bars and cafés, so in theory you don't have to tip. However, it is polite when paying for drinks to round up the total and to leave one to five euros after a meal, depending on the quality of the service and the restaurant concerned.

FINE DINING

At the high end, Michelin-starred restaurants range from being gloriously old-fashioned, with truffle-studded foie gras terrines and venison in grand old sauces, to being acrobatically cutting-edge (at the time of printing Paris has 10 restaurants with three stars). One of the best ways to enjoy such restaurants is to opt for the

Les Cocottes serves its dishes in cast-iron pots, hence its name

chef's tasting menu (*dégustation*), which gets you a host of dishes in smaller-than-usual portions. Quite a few of the top-notch addresses serve fixed lunch menus that are significantly cheaper than the à la carte options – but their popularity means you'll need to book weeks in advance. Getting a table at any currently fashionable restaurant, for that matter, can present the same challenge.

Generally speaking, restaurants serve lunch from noon to 2.30 or 3pm and dinner from around 7 or 8 to 10.30 or 11pm, although this may vary, particularly in August, when many places shut for the summer.

GLOBAL CUISINE

If you get to the point where you think you might burst if you look at another plate of French food, take a break at one of the city's international restaurants. Paris is especially good for food

The iconic Art Deco La Coupole

from Morocco, Thailand, Vietnam and Japan. The greatest concentration of Chinese and Vietnamese restaurants is in the 5th and 13th *arrondissements* (roughly speaking, the Latin Quarter and south-east to the new Left Bank), and Japanese restaurants are numerous in parts of the 1st (especially on and around rue Ste-Anne). The best Moroccan restaurants are dotted across the capital, but the area around the Bastille is a good place to start. There is also excellent Lebanese food to be found in the 8th and 16th *arrondissements* (Madeleine, Grands Boulevards, Champs-Élysées and West).

EATING OUT WITH CHILDREN

Taking your children out to a restaurant should not be a problem, although you should check beforehand with the more upmarket places. French children are used to eating out from an early age, and are therefore generally well-behaved in restaurants. Many establishments offer a children's menu. If not, they may split a *prix fixe* menu between two. With very young children, just request an extra plate and give them food from your own. With the bread that should come automatically to a French table, and ice-cream or fruit to follow, most children will be well fed.

TO HELP YOU ORDER

Do you have a table? **Avez-vous une table?**
The bill, please **L'addition, s'il vous plaît**
I would like ... **J'aimerais...**

tea **du thé**
coffee **un café**
milk **du lait**
sugar **du sucre**
wine **du vin**
beer **une bière**
water **de l'eau**
bread **du pain**
butter **du beurre**
cheese **du fromage**
chips (fries) **des frites**
salt **du sel**

pepper **du poivre**
salad **de la salade**
soup **de la soupe**
fish **du poisson**
seafood **des fruits de mer**
meat **de la viande**
very rare **bleu**
rare **saignant**
medium-rare **rose**
medium **à point**
well done **bien cuit**

MENU READER

agneau lamb
ail garlic
bœuf beef
canard duck
champignons mushrooms
chou cabbage
crevettes roses/grises
   prawns/shrimps
épinards spinach
escargots snails
fraises strawberries
haricots verts green beans
huîtres oysters
jambon ham

moules mussels
œufs eggs
oignons onions
petits pois peas
poire pear
pomme apple
pomme de terre potato
porc pork
poulet chicken
riz rice
saucisse sausage
saumon salmon
thon tuna
veau veal

PLACES TO EAT

We have used the following symbols to give an idea of the price for a three-course meal for one, including half a bottle of house wine, tax and service:

€€€€   over 60 euros
€€€   40–60 euros
€€   25–50 euros
€   under 25 euros

THE ISLANDS

Auberge de la Reine Blanche €€ *30, rue Saint Louis en l'Ile, tel: 01 85 15 21 30*, www.aubergedelaraineblanche.fr. Fri–Tues noon–2.30pm, 6.15–10pm, Thu 6.30-9.30pm. This long-established little restaurant creates a homely atmosphere with bistro-style chairs and tables and copper pans hanging from the wood-beamed ceiling. The regularly changing menu offers classics such as *soup à l'oignon*, *coq au vin* and *tarte tatin*.

THE RIGHT BANK
Louvre and Tuileries

Le Fumoir €€€ *6 rue de l'Amiral-de-Coligny, tel: 01 42 92 00 24;* www.lefumoir.com. Open daily 11am–2am. Facing the Louvre, spacious, sophisticated Le Fumoir is renowned for shaking some of the best cocktails in town. It serves light pan-European cooking, such as poached cod with a warm salad of fennel, tomatoes and olives.

Le Grand Véfour €€€€ *17 rue de Beaujolais, tel: 01 42 96 56 27;* www.grand-vefour.com. Open for lunch and dinner Mon–Fri. Set under the arches of the Palais-Royal, this is one of the most beautiful restaurants in Paris. Le Grand Véfour opened its doors in 1784 and has fed the likes of Emperor Napoleon and writers Alphonse Lamartine and Victor Hugo. Today it serves haute cuisine in the hands of chef Guy Martin.

Café Marly €€€€ *Palais du Louvre, 93 rue de Rivoli, tel: 01 49 26 06 60;* www.cafe-marly.com. Open for breakfast, lunch and dinner daily from 8am until 2am. Rest from your labours at the Louvre in the lavish Second Empire-style rooms facing the Pyramid, or on the attractive covered terrace. The food is modern European, the service sometimes a bit slow.

The Grands Boulevards

Chartier € *7 rue du Faubourg-Montmartre, tel: 01 47 70 86 29;* www.bouillon-chartier.com. Daily 11.30am until midnight; arrive before 1pm or before 8pm at night or you may not get a seat. The ambience at this historic budget option is an experience in itself: Belle Epoque decor, snappy waiters, shared tables and plenty of bonhomie.

Drouant €€€ *16-18 place Gaillon, tel: 01 42 65 15 16,* www.drouant.com. Open daily for lunch and dinner, this literary institution (the headquarters of the Goncourt and Renaudot prizes since 1914) is run by famed chef, Antoine Westermann and serves traditional French fare with a modern twist. Excellent wine list.

L'Opéra €€€€ *Palais Garnier, entrance on place Jacques Rouché, tel: 01 42 68 86 80;* www.opera-restaurant.fr. Daily 8am–midnight. With its two-storey undulating glass front, space-age interior with bright red chairs and carpets and, most of all, its location inside the Palais Garnier – the first time a restaurant has been set up here – this is one of the most talked-about restaurants in Paris. Splash out on miso-marinated black cod, kohlrabi with saffron and daikon turnip, or slide up to the bar for one of the sumptuous cocktails.

Café de la Paix €€€€ *5 place de l'Opéra, tel: 01 40 07 36 36;* www.cafedelapaix.fr. Open for breakfast, lunch and dinner daily. Its prices are steep, but this is one of the city's most historic cafés (it opened in 1862), and it is convenient for the Palais Garnier opposite and the department stores on boulevard Haussmann. There is a family-friendly brunch on Sundays.

Willi's Wine Bar €€€ *13 rue des Petits-Champs, tel: 01 42 61 05 09;* www.williswinebar.com. Open for lunch and dinner, Mon–Sat. In business for over 30 years, this classy establishment near the Palais Garnier is great for a full-blown meal à table or simply a glass of wine at its high oak bar.

Beaubourg, Marais, Bastille and East

L'As du Fallafel € *34 rue des Rosiers, tel: 01 48 87 63 60.* Open 11am–midnight Sun–Thu and until 5pm on Fri. The best *falafel* in Paris is a meal in itself. There are also *shawarma* sandwiches in pitta bread. Great location in the heart of the Marais.

Brasserie Bofinger €€€€ *5–7 rue de la Bastille, tel: 01 42 72 87 82;* www. bofingerparis.com. Open for lunch and dinner Mon–Sat, Sun dinner only. Close to the Opéra Bastille, the huge (300-seater) Bofinger is the archetypal Belle Epoque brasserie, complete with lush red-and-gold decor. It is a great place in which to enjoy delicious oysters and seafood, and specialities from Alsace such as *choucroute.*

Chai 33 €€€ *33 cour St-Emilion, tel: 01 53 44 01 01;* www.chai33.com. Open for breakfast, lunch and dinner daily. This restaurant is set in a light, airy former wine warehouse with a view of Bercy park. Choose your wine according to six styles, from light with a bite to rich and silky, with refreshing fusion food to match. Unpretentious *sommeliers* are on hand to help with wine choices.

Le Chateaubriand €€€€ *129 avenue Parmentier, 75011; tel: 01 43 57 45 95;* www.lechateaubriand.net. Open for dinner only Tue–Sat. This 'néo-bistrot' headed up by acclaimed chef, Iñaki Aizpitarte, has been awarded a Michelin star and is consistently voted in the top 10 of best restaurants in the world. Daily changing menu. Book well in advance.

Chez Omar €€ *47 rue de Bretagne, tel: 01 42 72 36 26.* Open for lunch Mon–Sat, for dinner daily. Couscous is one of the most popular international dishes in Paris, and this perennially popular address does some of the best. It doesn't take bookings, so you will have to get there early or join the queue outside. The portions are hearty, and the roast lamb is superb.

Chez Prune €€ *36 rue Beaurepaire, tel: 01 42 41 30 47.* Open for lunch and dinner daily. This is a cornerstone of the trendy Canal St-Martin area, and a great spot from which to watch the world go by. Good food at lunchtime; tapas-style snacks at night.

Le Petit Fer à Cheval €€ *30 rue Vieille-du-Temple, tel: 01 42 72 47 47;* www.cafeine.com. Open for lunch and dinner daily. With its tiny horse-shoe-shaped bar, this café on the Marais's trendy rue Vieille-du-Temple, is atmospheric and a great favourite with the bourgeois-bohemian crowd. Decent food. Friendly service.

Le Square Trousseau €€€ *1 rue Antoine-Vollon, tel: 01 43 43 06 00;* www.squaretrousseau.com. Daily 8am–2am. A spacious bistro with Art Deco lamps, colourful tiles, a glamorous bar and terrace facing a leafy square. Among the delights available are gazpacho, tuna tartare, rosemary lamb and spring vegetables, beef with shallot sauce, and raspberry gratin.

Le Train Bleu €€€€ *Gare de Lyon, tel: 01 43 43 09 06;* www.le-train-bleu.com. Open for lunch and dinner daily. Built over a century ago, this huge restaurant in the Gare de Lyon is an artistic marvel, with frescoed ceilings and Belle Epoque murals. Classic French dishes are efficiently served. Good-value set menus. There is also a bar.

Végét'Halles €€ *41 rue des Bourdonnais, tel: 01 40 41 93 95;* http://vegethalles.fr. Open Mon–Sat for lunch and dinner. Good-value vegetarian and vegan restaurant south east of Les Halles. The menu includes salads, mushroom roast with blackberry and ginger sauce and there is a good choice of desserts such as fruit crumble or chocolate and banana cake.

Champs-Élysées and Trocadéro

Alain Ducasse au Plaza Athénée €€€€ *25 avenue Montaigne, tel: 01 58 00 22 43;* www.alainducasse-plazaathenee.com. Open for lunch Thu–Fri, dinner Mon–Fri. Here, cooking has been elevated to an art form, by one of only two chefs in the world to hold 21 Michelin stars throughout his career (three of which are held by the Plaza). Expect truffles in abundance and superb vegetables from Provence. Reserve well ahead.

L'Entredgeu €€ *83 rue Laugier, tel: 01 40 54 97 24;* www.lentredgeu.fr. Open for lunch and dinner Mon–Fri, dinner only on Sat. The unpronounceable name and non-central location apart, this superior bistro has a lot going for it. Dishes include roast duckling in honey sauce and lots of foie gras, and the decor is suitably cosy and intimate.

Le Pavillon Elysée Lenôtre €€€ *10 avenue des Champs-Élysées, 75008;* tel: 01 42 65 85 10; www.lenotre.com. Open for lunch and dinner Mon–Fri. This pâtisserie is opposite the Grand Palais, in a glass pavilion created for the 1900 World Fair. The main reason to come here is for the delicious cakes, for which Lenôtre is best known. It's also possible to have a three-course meal.

Western Paris

Pré Catelan €€€€ *Bois de Boulogne, tel: 01 44 14 41 14;* http://restaurant. leprecatelan.com. Open for lunch and dinner Tue–Sat, lunch only on Sun. This is one of the most romantic spots in Paris, situated in the heart of the Bois de Boulogne. Haute cuisine, centring on fresh truffles, lobster, lamb and fresh seafood. Book well ahead.

Montmartre and the Northeast

Le Coq Rico €€€€ *98 rue Lepic, tel: 01 42 59 82 89;* www.lecoqrico. com. Open daily for lunch and dinner. If you love poultry then this smart restaurant from Antoine Westermann is the place to come. Try roast chicken accompanied by homemade chips. The *plat du jour* (€15) changes daily.

Rose Bakery €€ *46 rue des Martyrs, tel: 01 42 82 12 80.* Open daily 9.30am–8.30pm. Considered a folly when it opened in 2002, this deli-style café run by a Franco-British couple quickly made its mark, and is still going strong. The ingredients are of the highest quality, and make the soups, salads and quiches really shine. Vegetarian options.

Chez Toinette €€€ *20 rue Germain-Pilon, tel: 01 42 54 44 36.* Open for dinner Mon–Sat. With its red walls and romantic lighting, this cosy and convivial bistro in the heights of Montmartre is a good bet for a classic French dinner. Try the wild boar terrine, and don't miss the superb crème brûlée.

THE LEFT BANK

Latin Quarter and St-Germain-des-Prés

L'Alcazar €€€ *62 rue Mazarine, tel: 01 53 10 19 99; www.alcazar.fr.* Open for lunch and dinner daily. Sir Terence Conran's contribution to the Paris restaurant scene was to transform this former music hall into a designer brasserie. It's been a hit, thanks to the easy-going atmosphere and competitively priced menu, which includes an upmarket interpretation of British fish and chips. DJs play on the mezzanine Tue–Sat.

L'Atelier de Joël Robuchon €€€€ *Hotel du Pont Royal, 5 rue Montalembert, tel: 01 42 22 56 56; www.joel-robuchon.net.* Open for lunch and dinner daily. Parisians queue up in all weathers to sample the warm *brochettes de foie gras,* or tapenade with fresh tuna conjured by Axel Manes, the Michelin-starred protégé of France's most revered chef. The two-star Michelin restaurant is set around an open kitchen, so you can watch the masters at work. A second Atelier can be found at Publicis Drugstore (www.publicisdrugstore.com) on the Champs-Élysées featuring set lunch menus. Gluten-free menu is also available.

Le Comptoir €€€ *Hôtel Le Relais St-Germain, 9 carrefour de l'Odéon, tel: 01 44 27 07 97; www.hotel-paris-relais-saint-germain.com.* Open for lunch and dinner daily. Since its launch in 2005, chef Yves Camdeborde's Art Deco restaurant – in the 17th century hotel he runs with his wife Claudine – has been a steady hit with the city's gastronomes. Queues at lunchtime say all you need to know about the superb updated brasserie fare, such as chicken *basquaise* or salmon croque-monsieur. Tables are tightly packed, and the atmosphere is always convivial. You'll need to book ahead for the set menu dinner.

La Ferrandaise €€€ *8 rue de Vaugirard, tel: 01 43 26 36 36;* www.lafer randaise.com. Open for lunch and dinner Mon–Fri, dinner only Sat. An old-fashioned red entrance sets the tone for this Left Bank restaurant, with its three atmospheric dining rooms boasting exposed beams and tiled floors. The food is traditional French: try the sardines cooked in lemon juice or the succulent Bresse chicken with morel mushrooms.

Guy Savoy €€€€ *Monnaie de Paris, 11 quai de Conti, tel: 01 43 80 40 61;* www.guysavoy.com. Open for lunch Tue–Fri, Sat dinner only. The son of a gardener, Guy Savoy has an obsession with vegetables that has anticipated the current trend by more than a decade. The Michelin-starred chef happily pairs truffles with lentils or artichokes, and regularly makes the rounds to greet his guests.

Polidor €€ *41 rue Monsieur-le-Prince, tel: 01 43 26 95 34;* www.polidor. com. Open for lunch and dinner daily. This bohemian restaurant is a perennial favourite of students and budget diners. The *plats du jour* have been reliable for around 150 years and arrive in hearty helpings. *Bœuf bourguignon* and *tarte tatin* are just the kind of traditional dishes to expect here.

Le Rostand €€€ *6 place Edmond-Rostand, tel: 01 43 54 61 58.* Open 8am–12.30am daily. This is one of the city's more upmarket cafés, with prices to match – but it's the sort of place you should treat yourself to at least once on a trip to Paris. A fine view of the Jardin du Luxembourg, good cocktails, a delicious snacks menu and an attractive mirrors-and-mahogany interior make this a classy spot for refreshment.

Around the Eiffel Tower

Au Bon Accueil €€€€ *14 rue de Monttessuy, tel: 01 47 05 46 11;* www.au bonaccueilparis.com. Open for lunch and dinner Mon–Fri. This elegant bistro serves modern classics. The *prix-fixe* dinner menu (around €36) is viewed by many locals as one of the best deals in the neighbourhood, and the wine list is excellent. Seats on the terrace have views of its near neighbour the Eiffel Tower.

Les Cocottes €€€ *135 rue St-Dominique,* www.maisonconstant.com. Open for lunch and dinner daily. This contemporary bistro run by chef Christian Constant has been packing Parisians in for its non-stop service of affordable and hearty grub: things like pumpkin soup or preserved shoulder of lamb. The name alludes to the cast-iron pots the food comes to the table in.

Le Jules Verne €€€€ *2nd floor, Eiffel Tower, tel: 01 45 55 61 44;* www.lejulesverne-paris.com. Open for lunch and dinner daily (closed for renovations and due to reopen in spring 2019). Location-wise, this restaurant on the second level of the Eiffel Tower is perfect for a celebration or romantic dinner, and since Alain Ducasse took over the nine-year concession in 2007, the food has improved considerably. Specialities include pan-seared turbot with violet artichokes and Provençal figs.

Montparnasse

La Closerie des Lilas €€€€ *171 boulevard du Montparnasse, tel: 01 40 51 34 50;* www.closeriedeslilas.fr. Open for lunch and dinner daily. This historic brasserie still has a lot of charm and richly satisfying fare, though it lives off its reputation as a watering hole in the 1920s – tables are inscribed with the names of clients Lenin, Modigliani and André Breton. A pianist plays in the evening.

La Coupole €€€ *102 boulevard du Montparnasse, tel: 01 43 20 14 20;* www.lacoupole-paris.com. Open for breakfast, lunch and dinner daily. Opened in 1927, this vast, iconic Art Deco brasserie, now run by the Flo Brasserie group, is still going strong. Brasserie fare includes huge platters of shellfish and grilled meats.

A–Z TRAVEL TIPS

A SUMMARY OF PRACTICAL INFORMATION

A

ACCOMMODATION (see also Hotel Listings on page 133)

Paris is a popular destination all year round, so booking in advance is always recommended, especially from May to September and during the two annual fashion weeks. Most hotels stay open in the quieter months, but booking ahead is still a good idea, as many establishments offer discounts or package deals.

For a long stay you might consider renting a serviced apartment; a list of addresses can be found at www.cityzenbooking.com or any number of homes available on **Airbnb** (www.airbnb.co.uk). Travel sections of national newspapers carry advertisements; the *International Herald Tribune* and Fusac (www.fusac.fr) list accommodation for rent. **Alcôve & Agapes** (tel: +33 6 99 44 75 75; www.bed-and-breakfast-in-paris.com) organise rooms in private homes.

> Do you have a single/double room? **Avez-vous une chambre pour une/deux personnes?**
> What's the rate per night? **Quel est le prix pour une nuit?**

AIRPORTS

Paris has two main international airports. **Roissy-Charles-de-Gaulle (CDG)**, 30km (19 miles) northeast, and **Orly (ORY)**, 18km (11 miles) south. For information on both, see www.parisaeroport.fr.

Charles-de-Gaulle to Central Paris

Train: The quickest way to central Paris from Roissy is by RER (line B) train. They leave every 7–8 minutes between 4.56am and 11.56pm from station Roissypole (for Terminal 1 and 3) and station CDG 2 (for Terminal 2) and run to the Métro stations at Gare du Nord and Châtelet, taking about 30 minutes. Tickets cost €10.30; the Passe Navigo Découverte is valid. See http://parisbytrain.com for info.

Bus: Roissybus (www.easycdg.com) runs to rue Scribe (near the Palais Garnier) from terminals 1, 2A-2C, 2D-2B, 2E-2F and 3 (bus station). The service runs every 15–20 minutes from 6.00am to 12.30am; journey time is 60 minutes. Tickets cost from €8.70 and the five-zone Passe Navigo Découverte is valid. Alternatively, Le Bus Direct (www.lebusdirect.com)runs daily every 30 minutes from CDG 1 and 2: the green-coded line 2 runs to Av de Suffren, near the Eiffel Tower, stopping near the Champs-Elysées and at the Trocadéro on the way (5.45am–11pm; 1hr 10min to the Eiffel Tower), while the orange-coded line 4 stops at Gare de Lyon before terminating near Gare Montparnasse (6am–10.30pm; 1hr 15 min to Montparnasse). Tickets cost from €17 one way. Magical Shuttle (http://magicalshuttle.co.uk) provides a direct service to Disneyland (€23).

Taxi: Can take anything from 30 minutes to over an hour. Fares are metered, with supplements charged for each large piece of luggage; expect to pay in the region of €40–70.

Orly to Central Paris

Train: Take the local bus from gate F at Orly Sud or arrivals gate G at Orly Ouest to RER station Pont de Rungis (line C). Trains stop at St-Michel Notre-Dame and Champ de Mars Tour Eiffel, running every 15 minutes from 5am to 11.30pm. The journey takes around 30 minutes. Tickets cost €2 for bus no. 183 (to Port de Choissy) and €6.15 for the RER; the four-zone RATP Navigo pass is valid. Alternatively, take the Orlyval shuttle train from gate K at Orly Sud or departure gate A at Orly Ouest to RER station Antony (line B). Trains stop at St Michel Notre-Dame, Châtelet Les Halles and Gare du Nord. Orlyval services run every 7 minutes from 6am to 11.35pm; the RER runs every 15 minutes. Journey time is about 30 minutes. A combined ticket costs €12.05, or €9.30 with a three-zone RATP Navigo pass.

Bus: The Orlybus runs to Métro Denfert-Rochereau from Orly Sud gate G or Orly Ouest arrivals gate D. It runs every 10–20 minutes from 6am to 12.30am. The trip takes around 30 minutes, and tickets cost €8; the four-zone RATP Navigo pass is valid.

The Bus Direct line 1 (www.lebusdirect.com) purple service runs daily from 6am–11.40pm, every 20 mins to Etoile/Champs Elysées, stopping at Gare Montparnasse, the Eiffel Tower and Trocadéro. The journey takes about 1hr to Etoile/Champs Elysées and costs €12 one way.

Taxi: The journey from Orly to the city centre takes 20–40 minutes; expect to pay in the region of €40–55.

Tram: Tramway 7 links the airport with Villejuif-Louis Aragon station (Metro line 7).

B

BICYCLE HIRE (RENTAL)

Cycling in Paris has been revolutionised by the city council's hugely successful Vélib' scheme (www.velib-metropole.fr), launched in 2007. Vélib' lets you pick up and return one of over 20,000 bikes (30 percent of which are electric) at any of 1,800 automated stations all over the city. A card valid for a week or a day can be bought from the stations, or online in advance. You then pay for each journey you make, according to its duration; trips under 30 minutes are free.

Alternatively, you can hire bikes and tandems by the day or week from Paris à Vélo C'est Sympa (22 rue Alphonse Bourdon, tel: 01 48 87 60 01; www.parisvelosympa.com); the company also operates guided cycle tours of the city.

BUDGETING FOR YOUR TRIP

The price of accommodation varies widely. You can get a double room in a small pension for under €100 a night, or you can pay over €500 in a luxury hotel. An average price, however, for an en-suite double room in a centrally located, comfortable hotel is around €100–160. Meals also cover a wide price range, but on average expect to pay around €40–60 for a three-course meal with a half-bottle of house wine (though set menus cut costs). In everyday cafés and bars, a single espresso usually costs in the region from €2, and a pint of lager about €6. The average entrance price to a national museum or gallery is about €8–12 (municipal museums are free).

C

CAMPING

The only campsite within inner Paris (there are many more in the Paris region, for details see http://en.parisinfo.com) is Camping de Paris – Bois de Boulogne (2 allée du Bord de l'Eau, 75016; tel: 01 45 24 30 00; www.campingparis.fr), which is open all year. The site has cottages, wood trailers and canvas tents for hire as well as 35 pitches for guests with their own tents.

CAR HIRE (RENTAL)

To rent a car you will need your driver's licence and passport, as well as a major credit card or a large deposit. The minimum age for renting cars is 21, and you must have held a licence for at least a year. Third-party insurance is compulsory; full cover is recommended.

Among the international car-hire firms operating in Paris are:

Avis, tel: 08 21 23 07 60, www.avis.fr.

Budget, tel: 08 25 00 35 64, www.budget.com.

easyCar, tel: 01 70 61 85 52, www.easycar.com.

Europcar, tel: 08 25 35 83 58, www.europcar.com.

Hertz, tel: 01 39 38 38 38 www.hertz.com.

CLIMATE

In winter temperatures in Paris average 4°C (39°F); in summer around 22°C (72°F). Spring and autumn tend to be mild, with an average of 11°C (52°F). June, September and October are ideal for visiting, as they are warm, usually sunny, but less stifling than mid-summer.

CLOTHING

Parisians tend to be dressier than Londoners or New Yorkers. In smarter restaurants men may be expected to wear jackets, although ties are rarely insisted upon. Wear decorous clothing at religious sites.

CRIME AND SAFETY

There are pickpockets in some Métro stations and at major tourist sites. Obvious centres of prostitution (such as rue St-Denis and parts of the Bois de Boulogne) are best avoided at night. It is always a good idea to keep a photocopy of your passport in case of theft. In the event of loss or theft, you'll need to make a report at the nearest police station (*commissariat de police*), which will be required if you wish to claim on your insurance.

Following the November 2015 attacks, expect extra security checks at airports and major attractions. Be aware that suitcases, travel bags and backpacks exceeding 55 x 35 x 25cm (21 x 14 x 10ins) will not be allowed in most museums and cannot be left at cloakrooms.

D

DRIVING

Driving in Paris requires confidence and concentration. Traffic drives on the right, seat belts are obligatory, and the speed limit in town is 50kph (30mph). Do not drive in bus lanes at any time, and give priority to vehicles approaching from the right. This applies to some roundabouts, where cars on the roundabout stop for those coming on to it. Most car parks are underground (see www.parkingsdeparis.com), and street parking is hard to find; spaces are usually metered Mon–Sat 9am–8pm (payment can only be made with a Paris Carte, €15 or €30 from local tabacs or using the PaybyPhone app), and maximum stay is two hours. Fuel can be hard to find in the city centre, so if your tank is almost empty head for a *porte* (exit) on the Périphérique (the multi-lane ring road), where petrol stations are open 24 hours a day. The complete list of addresses can be found on the tourist office website (see page 129).

Drivers are liable to heavy on-the-spot fines for speeding and drink driving. The drink limit in France is 50mg/litre of alcohol in the blood (equivalent to about two glasses of wine), and is strictly enforced.

If you break down, contact Europ Assistance (tel: 01 41 85 85 85), but expect to pay a high cost unless you have already taken out its insurance cover.

driver's licence **permis de conduire**
car registration papers **carte grise**
Yield to traffic from right **Priorité à droite**
Slow down **Ralentir**
Keep right/left **Serrez à droite/à gauche**
One way **Sens unique**
Give way **Cédez ta priorité/le passage**

E

ELECTRICITY
You'll need an adapter: French sockets have two round holes. Supplies are 220 volt, and US equipment will need a transformer.

EMBASSIES AND CONSULATES
Australia 4 rue Jean-Rey, 75724; tel: 01 40 59 33 00; www.france.embassy.gov.au
Canada 130 rue du Faubourg Saint-Honoré, 75008; tel: 01 44 43 29 00; www.canadainternational.gc.ca/france
New Zealand 103 rue de Grenelle, 75007; tel: 01 45 01 43 43; www.nzembassy.com/france
Republic of Ireland Embassy: 12 avenue Foch, 75116; tel: 01 44 17 67 00; www.embassyofireland.fr

South Africa 59 quai d'Orsay, 75343; tel: 01 53 59 23 23; www.afriquesud.net
UK Embassy: 35 rue du Faubourg-St-Honoré, 75383; tel: 01 44 51 31 00; www.gov.uk/world/organisations/british-embassy-paris.
US Embassy: 2 avenue Gabriel, 75008; tel: 01 43 12 22 22; http:// usem bassy.gov.

EMERGENCIES
Ambulance (SAMU) 15
Police (*police secours*) 17
Fire brigade (*sapeurs-pompiers*) 18
From a mobile phone: 112

Fire! **Au feu!**
Help! **Au secours!**

G

GETTING THERE (see also Airports)
By Air: Air France is the main agent for flights to France from the US and within Europe and also handles bookings for some of the smaller operators, such as HOP!. For British travellers, operators such as British Airways (www.ba.com) and the low-cost airlines easyJet (www.easyjet.com), Flybe (www.flybe.com) and Jet2 (www.jet2.com) offer flights to Paris from London and other British cities. See www.skyscanner.net to compare prices.
By Rail: The Eurostar is the most convenient way to get to Paris (Gare du Nord) from the UK, with fast, frequent rail services from London (St Pancras International), Ebbsfleet and Ashford. The service runs about 12 times a day and takes two and a quarter hours (two hours from Ebbsfleet). For reservations, contact Eurostar on tel: 0343 218 6186 (UK) or 08 92 35 35 39 (France), or visit www.eurostar.com. There are reduced fares for children aged 4–11.
By Car: Eurotunnel takes cars and passengers from Folkestone to Calais

on Le Shuttle. It takes 35 minutes from platform to platform and about one hour from motorway to motorway. You can book in advance with Eurotunnel on tel: 0844 879 7371 (UK) or 08 10 63 03 04 (France) or at www.eurotunnel.com or just turn up and take the next available service. Le Shuttle runs 24 hours a day, all year, and there are between two and five an hour.

By Bus: National Express subsidiary Eurolines runs daily services from London (Victoria Coach Station) to Paris (Métro Gallieni), providing one of the cheaper ways to get there. For more information, tel: 0871 781 81778 (UK) or 08 92 89 90 91 (France), or visit www.eurolines.eu.

GUIDES AND TOURS

Find multilingual guides and interpreters through the tourist office (see page 129). One of the best suppliers of guided tours is Paris Walks, which has been going for nearly 20 years; see www.paris-walks.com. To save shoe leather, try a tour on a Segway - see www.fattiretours.com for more details.

H

HEALTH AND MEDICAL CARE (see also Emergencies)

EU Nationals: EU nationals can receive emergency medical treatment. You will have to pay, but can claim from the French Sécurité Sociale, which refunds up to 70 per cent of your medical bill. You must have a European Health Insurance Card (www.ehic.org.uk).

North American Citizens: Contact the International Association for Medical Assistance to Travellers (iamat), tel: 416 652 0137 (Canada) or 716 754 4883 (US), www.iamat.org. This non-profit group offers members fixed rates for medical treatment from participating physicians.

English-speaking health services are at the American Hospital, tel: 01 46 41 25 25, www.american-hospital.org, and the Hertford British Hospital, tel: 01 46 21 46 46, www.british-hospital.org.

Chemists: Pharmacies can be identified by their green (usually neon-lit) 'plus' sign. Pharmacie des Halles (10 boulevard de Sébastopol, Métro

Châtelet; tel: 01 42 72 03 23) is open 8am–9pm, Mon-Sat. La Pharmacie de la Place de la République (5, place de la République, Métro République; tel: 0 1 47 00 18 08) is open 7 days a week, 24 hours a day.

L

LGBTQ TRAVELLERS

The city has a large, visible and quite relaxed LGBTQ community. Gay bars and clubs are concentrated in the Marais. The magazine *Têtu*, available at kiosks, is a useful source of information (in French). For more information see the following websites in English: www.paris-marais.com, www.gay-france.net and http://paris.gaycities.com.

LOST PROPERTY

If you lose your passport, report it to your consulate (see page 122 or search for 'Ambassades et Consulats' on www.pagesjaunes.fr).

If your credit card is lost or stolen, the numbers to ring are:

American Express, tel: +44 12 73 69 69 33

Mastercard, tel: +44 19 28 58 44 21

Visa, tel: 01 30 52 78 42 85

To reclaim anything else you have lost, you should go (with ID) to the Bureau des Objets Trouvés (36 rue des Morillons, Métro Convention; tel: 01 53 71 53 71; open Mon–Wed 8.30am–5pm, Thu 8.30am–noon, Fri 8.30am–4.30pm). You can contact them via their website (www.prefecturedepolice.interieur.gouv.fr) or to visit the office in person.

M

MAPS

Paris Pratique par Arrondissement, an indexed, pocket-sized street atlas, is the most useful map for visitors. It can be bought for around €6 at newsstands and kiosks. Most Métro stations supply free, decent maps of the Métro system, bus network and RER train system.

MEDIA

Newspapers: The two main national dailies are *Le Monde*, which has a left-ish slant, and the more conservative *Le Figaro*. The local daily is *Le Parisien*. British, American and other European dailies are widely available on the same day at city-centre kiosks and shops showing 'journaux' or 'presse' signs. The US-flavoured Fusac (www.fusac.fr) is a free fortnightly English-language magazine containing job offers, classified ads and some event information; it is available in Anglo-themed bars and restaurants.

Radio: France Inter (87.8 MHz) is the main national radio station, with a mix of serious discussion, culture and humour. RTL (104.3 MHz) is the most popular station throughout France, playing music from the charts, interspersed with chat shows.

Television: TF1, France 2, France 3, Canal+, France 5, Arte and M6 are the six main television stations on offer.

MONEY

Currency: The euro (€) is divided into 100 cents (¢ or ct). Coins (*pièces*) come in 1, 2, 5, 10, 20 and 50 cents, and 1 and 2 euros. Banknotes (*billets*) come in 5, 10, 20, 50, 100, 200 and 500 euros. ATMs are widespread, and accept most of the major international debit and credit cards; check withdrawal charges with your bank before you go.

Banks and currency exchange offices (banque; bureau de change): Take your passport when changing money or travellers' cheques. Your hotel may offer an exchange service, though at a worse rate.

Travellers' cheques: These are widely accepted (with identification).

I want to change some pounds/dollars **Je voudrais changer des livres sterling/dollars**
Do you accept travellers' cheques/this credit card? **Acceptez-vous les chèques de voyage/cette carte de crédit?**

O

OPENING HOURS

Traditionally, banks open Mon–Fri 9am–5pm and close at the weekend, though many now open on Saturday morning and close on Monday. Food shops tend to open early. Traditionally, most shops close for lunch, but in Paris, many remain open, closing at 7 or 7.30pm. The larger department stores do not close at lunchtime and are open until 9 or 10pm on Thursday. Most shops close on Sunday; many museums close on Monday or Tuesday and ticket offices usually shut at least 30 minutes prior to the official closing time.

P

POLICE (see also Emergencies)

The blue-uniformed police who keep law and order and direct traffic are, as a general rule, courteous and helpful to visitors. The CRS (*Compagnies républicaines de sécurité*) are the tough guys, brought in for demonstrations. The main police station is the Préfecture de Police, at 1 Rue de Lutèce (tel: 34 30; www.prefecture-police-paris.interieur.gouv.fr).

If you need to call for police help, dial 17 (anywhere in France).

Where is the nearest police station? **Où se trouve le commissariat de police le plus proche?**

POST OFFICES

The French postal service is run by La Poste (www.laposte.fr). Main post offices are open Mon–Fri 8am–7pm, Sat 8am–noon. The central post office (16 rue Etienne Marcel, tel: 36 31) operates a 24-hour service. Stamps (*timbres*) are available at most tobacconists (*tabacs*). Post boxes are yellow.

PUBLIC HOLIDAYS

Public offices, banks and most shops close on public holidays, though you will find the odd corner shop open.

1 January *Jour de l'An* New Year's Day
1 May *Fête du Travail* Labour Day
8 May *Fête de la Victoire* Victory Day (1945)
14 July *Fête Nationale* Bastille Day
15 August *Assomption* Assumption
1 November *Toussaint* All Saints' Day
11 November *Armistice* Armistice Day (1918)
25 December *Noël* Christmas Day
Moveable dates:
Pâques Easter
Lundi de Pâques Easter Monday
Ascension Ascension Day
Lundi de Pentecôte Whit Monday

T

TELEPHONES

Telephone numbers in France have 10 digits. Paris and Île de France numbers begin with 01; toll-free phone numbers begin with 0800; other numbers beginning with 08 are charged at variable rates; 06 numbers are mobile numbers. There are coin-operated (rare) and card-operated phone boxes in Paris. Calls are usually cheaper between 9pm and 9am on weekdays, and from 2pm at weekends. A *télécarte* can be bought at various prices from kiosks, tabacs and post offices. You can also dial from all post offices. Cafés and tabacs often have public phones.

UK mobile phones will work in Paris. For long stays, you can buy a pay-as-you-go (*sans abonnement*) mobile phone from Orange (www.orange.fr), SFR (www.sfr.fr), Bouygues Telecom (www.bouyguestelecom.fr) or Free (http://mobile.free.fr), all of whom have shops on French high streets.

Direct Dialling to Paris from the UK: 00 (international code) + 33

(France) + 1 (Paris) + an eight-figure number. To call abroad from France, dial the international access code (00), then the country code.
Directory Enquiries: 118 218, 32 12 (international enquiries).
Operator: 3123

TIME DIFFERENCES

France keeps to Central European Time (GMT +1 hour; GMT +2 hours Apr–Oct). When it is noon in Paris, it is 11am in London, 6am in New York, 10pm in Auckland, 8pm in Sydney and noon in Johannesburg.

What time is it? **Quelle heure est-il?**

TIPPING

By law, restaurant bills must include the service charge, usually 12 or 15 percent. Nevertheless, it is common to leave a small additional tip (around 5 per cent) for the waiter, if the service has been good. With taxis, it is usual to round up to the nearest euro.

TOILETS

There are some 400 automated public toilets (*sanisettes*) parked on pavements across the city; all are clearly marked. They are unisex, disinfected after each use, and free of charge. Most cafés have toilets, although these are, in principle, reserved for their customers.

TOURIST INFORMATION

The main Paris tourism authority is the Office du Tourisme de Paris, www.parisinfo.com. Branches are listed below.
In the UK: ATOUT France, 300 High Holborn, London WC1V 7JHL, tel: 020 70 61 66 31, www.atout-france.fr.
In the US: ATOUT France, 825 Third Avenue, 29th floor, NY-10022; tel: 212 838 78 00, www.atout-france.fr.

In Canada: 1800 avenue McGill Collège, Bureau 1010, Montréal, Québec, H3A 3J6; tel: 514 288 2026; http://ca.france.fr.

In Australia: French Tourist Bureau, Level 13, 25 Bligh Street, 2000 NSW, Sydney; tel: 61 2 92 31 62 77; http://au.france.fr.

In Paris: Pyramides: 25 rue des Pyramides, 75001. Daily 9am–7pm (from 10am Nov–Apr). Gare du Nord: 18 rue de Dunkerque, 75010. Daily 8am–6pm. Gare de Lyon: 20 boulevard Diderot, 75012. Mon–Sat 8am–6pm. Gare de l'Est: place du 11 novembre 1918, 75010. Mon–Sat 8am–7pm. Anvers: 72 boulevard de Rochechouart, 75018. Daily 10am–6pm.

TRANSPORT

All public transport in Paris is run by the Régie Autonome des Transports Parisiens (RATP; tel: 32 46; www.ratp.fr). There is an information office at 54 quai de la Rapée, 75012 Paris.

Bus (autobus): Bus transport around Paris is efficient, though not always fast. You can obtain a bus route plan from Métro station ticket counters. Most buses run 7am–8.30pm, some until 12.30am. Service is reduced on Sundays and public holidays. Special Noctilien services (www.noctilien.fr) operate on over 45 routes across the capital and suburbs, from 12.30am–5.30am every hour, with Châtelet as the hub.

Bus journeys take one ticket. You can buy a ticket as you board, but it is cheaper to buy a book of tickets (carnet) from any Métro station or tobacconist. Punch your ticket in the validating machine when you get on. You can also buy special one-, three- or five-day tourist passes or the weekly ticket and Navigo (see page 131). Show these special tickets to the driver as you get on, rather than putting them in the punching machine. The fine for being caught without a ticket is €5 (or €30 for deferred payment).

Métro: The Paris Métropolitain ('Métro') is fast, efficient and inexpensive. You get 10 journeys (including connections) for the price of seven with a carnet (book) of tickets. Tickets are also valid for the bus network and for the RER (in zones 1-2). Keep your ticket until you exit the station. A special ticket called **_Paris Visite_**, valid for one, three or five days, allows unlimited travel on the bus or Métro, and reductions on entrance fees to various attractions. A day ticket, **Mobilis**, is valid for the Métro, RER, buses, suburban trains and some airport buses. For longer stays, the best buy is a **Navigo** smart card, valid for unlimited rides inside Paris on the Métro and bus, either weekly (*hebdomadaire*) Mon–Sun, monthly (*mensuel*), or annual (*annuel*). Have a passport photo ready.

Métro stations have big, easy-to-read maps. Services start at 6am and finish around 1am (last trains leave end stations at 12.30am).

Train: The SNCF (French railway authority) is fast, comfortable and efficient. The **high-speed service** (TGV) is excellent but more expensive (www.sncf.com or www.voyages-sncf.com). Make sure you validate (*composter*) your train ticket before boarding by inserting it in one of the orange machines on the way to the platform.

Taxi: Taxis are reasonably priced, though there are extra charges for putting luggage in the boot and for pick-up at a station or airport. Taxi drivers can refuse to carry more than three passengers. The fourth, when admitted, pays a supplement.

You will find taxis cruising around or at stands, but finding an empty one can take time, especially at busy times. You can recognise an unoccupied cab by an illuminated sign on its roof. Fares differ according to the zones covered or the time (you'll be charged more between 7pm and 7am and on Sunday). A fare between Roissy-Charles-de-Gaulle Airport and central Paris can be up to €50 by day, €60 at night.

The following taxi companies take phone bookings 24 hours a day:
Alpha: 01 45 85 85 85; www.alphataxis.fr.
G7: 36 07; www.g7.fr. Also available as an app.

TRAVELLERS WITH DISABILITIES

The Paris Tourist Bureau (www.parisinfo.com) lists several companies (usually pharmacies) that rent wheelchairs and mobility scooters, such as Bastide le Confort Medical (39 rue Hermel, tel: 01 53 92 52 52; www.bastideleconfortmedical.com). **G7** is one of the few taxi companies to have a fleet of wheelchair accessible vehicles. Wheelchair users can visit Paris on Wheels, www.parisonwheels.com, for guided tours.

Useful Organisations
France: Association des Paralysés de France, Service Information, 17 blvd Auguste Blanqui, 75013; tel 01 40 78 69 00; www.apf-francehandicap.org.
UK: Disability Rights UK, Plexal, 14 East Bay Lane, London E20 3BS; tel: 0330 995 0400; www.disabilityrightsuk.org.
US: Society for Accessible Travel and Hospitality (SATH), 347 Fifth Ave., Suite 605, New York, NY 10016; tel: 212 447 7284; www.sath.org.

VISAS AND ENTRY REQUIREMENTS

Nationals of EU countries need a valid passport or identity document. Nationals from Australia, Canada, New Zealand and the US need passports; South African nationals need a visa: contact Consulat de France, Standard Bank Building, 3rd Floor, 191 Jan Smuts Avenue, Cnr 7th Avenue, Parktown North 2196, Johannesburg; tel: 011 778 56 00; www.johannesburg.consulfrance.org.

WEBSITES

www.paris.fr General information on Paris from the city council
www.parisinfo.com Paris official tourism site
www.parisvoice.com Online magazine about Paris for English speakers

YOUTH HOSTELS

A free guide to French youth hostels is available from the Fédération Unie des Auberges de Jeunesse (FUAJ), 20 rue Pajol, 75018 Paris; tel: 01 40 89 87 90; www.fuaj.org. Tourist information offices offer a booklet, *Jeunes à Paris* (Young People in Paris), listing details of hostels, student halls and other types of low-budget accommodation.

RECOMMENDED HOTELS

This list is divided geographically, covering hotels on the islands and the Right and Left banks. Note that the numbers in the postcode indicate the *arrondissement* (district), so 75004 is the 4th *arrondissement*.

Hotels on the islands are mainly small and old-fashioned, and few have lifts. Around the Louvre and Tuileries are some of the city's star addresses, such as the Ritz; further north, on and around the Grands Boulevards, are unassuming establishments with modern amenities. Try Beaubourg, Marais or Bastille for a crop of modern boutique hotels.

Western Paris offers full-on luxury. Montmartre hotels, on the other hand, tend to capitalise on the Butte's romantic reputation, but often nakedly angle their rates at the tourist crowd.

On the Left Bank, the Latin Quarter and St-Germain-des-Prés have chic, elegant and traditional establishments, but staying here is rarely cheap. You almost always pay a premium around the Eiffel Tower too. There are a few pleasant addresses to be found in Montparnasse.

The following ranges give an idea of the price for an en-suite double room per night. Service and tax are included; generally, breakfast is not.

€€€€	over 300 euros
€€€	200–300 euros
€€	100–200 euros
€	55–100 euros

THE ISLANDS

Hôtel des Deux-Îles €€€ *59 rue St-Louis-en-l'Île, 75004; tel: 01 43 26 13 35; www.deuxiles-paris-hotel.com.* Set in a small and attractive 17th century mansion on the main street of the tranquil Île St-Louis, this hotel, with just 17 rooms, is comfortable and friendly, with a cellar bar and a vaulted breakfast room with stone walls. Rooms are compact but nicely decorated. Wi-fi.

Hôtel du Jeu de Paume €€€€ *54 rue St-Louis-en-l'Île, 75004; tel: 01 43 26 14 18;* www.jeudepaumehotel.com. This 30-room Île St-Louis hotel is decorated in chic contemporary style, but has kept its 17th century *jeu de paume* (the original game of tennis) court. Wi-fi.

Hôtel de Lutèce €€€ *65 rue St-Louis-en-l'Île, 75004; tel: 01 43 26 23 52;* www.paris-hotel-lutece.com. This lovely Île St-Louis hotel is under the same management as the Deux-Îles (see page 133). It has 23 tiny, attractive and quiet rooms, several with exposed wooden beams. Those on the sixth floor are the most romantic. Wi-fi.

THE RIGHT BANK
Louvre and Tuileries

Hôtel Costes €€€€ *239-241 rue St-Honoré, 75001; tel: 01 42 44 50 00;* www.hotelcostes.com. This super-hip hotel is just off elegant place Vendôme in an exclusive neighbourhood lined with chic boutiques. The rooms are exquisitely decorated with Baroque paintings, heavy drapes and antiques. Some bathrooms have claw-foot bathtubs and mosaic tiles. Owner Jean-Louis Costes dislikes artificial light, so the hallways are lit with candles; even the beautiful indoor pool is dark.

Grand Hotel du Palais Royal €€€€ *4 rue de Valois, 75001; tel: 01 42 96 15 35;* www.grandhoteldupalaisroyal.com. This intimate luxury hotel is located in an 18th century building in the south eastern corner of the elegant Palais Royal. The 68 rooms and suites, some with their own balcony, successfully marry classical style with contemporary lines. As well as a restaurant and bar, there is also a spa, which uses Carita products and has its own hammam.

Hôtel Mansart €€€ *5 rue des Capucines, 75001; tel: 01 42 61 50 28;* www.paris-hotel-mansart.com. With some of the 57 rooms overlooking place Vendôme, this four-star hotel, named after the architect of Versailles, is a bargain for this area. Rooms are decorated in traditional style, furnished with antiques, yet have a contemporary feel and some have accessibility for people with reduced mobility. Museum passes available to buy.

The Grands Boulevards

Buddha Bar Hotel €€€€ *4 rue d'Anjou, 75008; tel: 01 83 96 88 88;* www.buddhabarhotelparis.com. A couple of streets west of place de la Madeleine and round the corner from the iconic Buddha Bar itself, is this Japanese-inspired, ultra-hip hotel .The 18th century building is lavishly decorated, the food is Pan Asian and the Quatre cocktail bar is intimate and elegant.

Hôtel Chopin € *46 passage Jouffroy, 75009; tel: 01 47 70 58 10;* www.hotelchopin-paris-opera.com. Set at the end of a historic 19th century glass-and-steel-roofed arcade, this is a quiet, friendly, simply furnished hotel. It is popular, too, so book well in advance. 36 rooms.

Hôtel Langlois €€ *63 rue St-Lazare, 75009; tel: 01 48 74 78 24;* www.hotel-langlois.com. If you fancy stepping back in time then this three-star hotel is the place for you. Rooms are decorated in Belle Epoque and Art Nouveau style, each furnished with antiques and paintings, each with original features dating from 1870 when the building was constructed.

W Paris – Opéra €€€€ *4 rue Meyerbeer, 75009; tel: 01 77 48 94 94;* www.marriott.com. In a grand 1870s building near the Opéra, this is the place to come if comfort is as important as style: the hotel is famous for its beds and all rooms have 40" TVs, rainforest showers and iPod docks. Chill out to the DJs in the W Lounge or try some gourmet food in the Coquette restaurant.

Beaubourg, Marais and Bastille

Hôtel Bourg Tibourg €€€ *19 rue du Bourg-Tibourg, 75004; tel: 01 42 78 47 39;* www.bourgtibourg.com. Situated on a charming narrow street in the heart of the Marais, this 17th century building is home to a well-kept, affordable boutique hotel stylishly decorated by celebrity designer Jacques Garcia in reds, blacks and Moroccan blues and golds. Breakfast is served in a vaulted dining room with exposed stone.

Le Citizen Hotel du Canal €€€ *96 quai de Jemmapes, 75010 tel: 01 83 62 55 50;* www.lecitizenhotel.com. In a lovely location next to the Canal

St-Martin, this eco-friendly, modern hotel has just 12 rooms, including two suites, with all mod cons including an iPad. There are regular art exhibitions and breakfast is included in the room price.

Hôtel Duo €€€ *11 rue du Temple, 75004; tel: 01 42 72 72 22;* www.duo-paris.com. This trendy hotel has an excellent location in the Marais. Rooms are furnished in contemporary style, with good-sized bathrooms. There is a bar downstairs, a courtyard garden and a gym.

Mama Shelter €€ *109 rue de Bagnolet, 75020; tel: 01 43 48 48 48;* www. mamashelter.com. This 170-room hotel has won a slew of awards for its looks, facilities, and value. The location is a fair distance east of Bastille, but the sleek Philippe Starck-designed rooms all come with iMacs, microwaves and free movies. Mama regularly hosts DJ sessions and its rooftop was voted 'best in Paris' by Vogue.

Pavillon de la Reine €€€€ *28 place des Vosges, 75003; tel: 01 40 29 19 19;* www.pavillon-de-la-reine.com. This romantic, stylish hotel, located on the beautiful place des Vosges, feels like a country château. Rooms vary greatly in size and price, but most have four-poster beds, exposed wooden beams and antiques. There is also a cosy lobby bar with evening wine-tasting, a spa, and manicured gardens.

Western Paris

Le Dokhan's A Tribute Portfolio Hotel €€€€ *117 rue de Lauriston, 75016; tel: 01 53 65 66 99;* www.hotelledokhansparis.com. This hotel in the Starwood chain has a fine western location with good views of the Eiffel Tower. The decor is classic luxury with contemporary touches: high ceilings, lots of wood and old-style fittings all set off by modern colours and warm lighting. There is a stylish champagne bar but no restaurant.

Saint James Paris €€€€ *43 avenue Bugeaud, 75016; tel: 01 44 05 81 81;* www.saint-james-paris.com. This outrageously luxurious mansion near Étoile was done out in 2011 by British interior designer Bambi Sloan in a sort of modern Baroque, complete with chandeliers. Among other glories, there is a drop-dead gorgeous library bar and a large garden dotted with kiosks made to look like Montgolfier balloons – whose real, historic predecessors used to take off here.

Montmartre

Chat Noir Design Hôtel €€ *68 boulevard de Clichy, 75018; tel: 01 42 64 15 26*; www.hotel-chatnoir-paris.com. The ubiquitous black cat image gives away this hotel location in the former famous nightclub of the same name. Rooms are white, bright and contemporary with splashes of red, black and yellow.

l'Ermitage Sacré-Coeur €€ *24 rue Lamarck, 75018; tel: 06 12 49 01 15*; www.ermitagesacrecoeur.fr. This 12-room hotel is located close to Sacré-Cœur in an old residential neighbourhood. It is a good budget choice, with friendly staff and colourful bedrooms decorated in French farmhouse style. No credit cards.

Terrass Hotel €€€ *12–14 rue Joseph de Maistre, 75018; tel: 01 46 06 72 85*; www.terrass-hotel.com. This Montmartre hotel has one considerable advantage over its rivals, in addition to its stylish decor and chic piano bar: the open-air lounge on its roof. Drinks and meals are served here in good weather, with panoramic views of the capital.

THE LEFT BANK
Latin Quarter and St-Germain-des-Prés

Abbaye St-Germain €€€€ *10 rue Cassette, 75006; tel: 01 45 44 38 11*; www.hotelabbayeparis.com. This 17th century abbey, attractively situated between the Jardin du Luxembourg and St-Germain-des-Prés, has been beautifully adapted into a hotel. A favourite haunt of writers and artists, the charm of the old decor has been maintained but there are all mod cons, and a lovely garden. Staff are helpful and attentive.

Hôtel d'Angleterre €€€ *44 rue Jacob, 75006; tel: 01 42 60 34 72*; www.hotel-dangleterre.com. The location could not be better, on a quiet, up-market street lined with art galleries. This lovely hotel was the site at which the Treaty of Paris, proclaiming the independence of the US, was signed in 1783; in the 19th century it was used as the British Embassy. Ernest Hemingway lodged here (in room 14) in 1921. Rooms are fairly small and furnished with antiques; only the top-floor doubles are spacious. Delightful terrace and garden.

Hôtel Familia €€ *11 rue des Ecoles, 75005; tel: 01 43 54 55 27; www.familia hotel.com.* Within a few minutes' walk of the islands and St-Germain-des-Prés, the Familia offers solid comforts in smallish rooms for a modest price; rooms on the fifth and sixth floors have views of Notre-Dame. Another attraction for the hotel's many regular guests is the hospitable Gaucheron family who live on the premises and take pride in every detail.

Hôtel des Grandes Ecoles €€ *75 rue du Cardinal-Lemoine, 75005; tel: 01 43 26 79 23; www.hotel-grandes-ecoles.com.* At first glance, you might think you were in the French countryside. There are 51 large, prettily furnished rooms around a cobbled courtyard and garden of established trees and trellised roses. Although it is a short uphill walk from the Métro, you are still near enough to attractions including rue Mouffetard. No TVs.

Hôtel de Nesle €€ *7 rue de Nesle, 75006; tel: 01 43 54 62 41; www.hotel denesleparis.com.* A laid-back students' and backpackers' hotel. Facilities are basic, but bedrooms are cheerfully decorated with murals, furnished to various eclectic themes and spotless. There is also a garden with a pond and an impressive palm tree.

Hotel Le Six €€€ *14 rue Stanislas, 75006; tel: 01 42 22 00 75; www.hotel-le-six.com.* Design-conscious but child-friendly boutique hotel, where the rooms have Nespresso machines and L'Occitane toiletries and some have balconies. Relax with a drink in the library lounge or winter garden, indulge in the signature 'Le Six' massage or ease away aches and pains in the hammam. No restaurant.

Around the Eiffel Tower

Amélie €€ *5 rue Amélie, 75007; tel: 01 45 51 74 75; www.hotelamelie-paris.com.* A short walk from the Eiffel Tower, this small, friendly, family-run hotel has some of the lowest rates in the area. Renovated rooms have small refrigerators and private bathrooms. A narrow wooden staircase leads up to the four levels of rooms; there is no lift. Breakfast is served in the small lobby.

Lenox St Germain €€ *9 rue de l'Université, 75007; tel: 01 42 96 10 95.* This trendy hotel is decorated in Art Deco style and is very popular among style-conscious types. There is a bar and the rooms are spotless. Reserve well in advance.

Hôtel Verneuil €€€ *8 rue de Verneuil, 75007; tel: 01 42 60 82 14; www.hotel-verneuil-saint-germain.com.* Lovely hotel in an elegant 17th century building in the upmarket 7th arrondissement, with small but attractive rooms renovated in contemporary style. Discreet service. Singer Serge Gainsbourg lived on this street, and the wall outside his old house is decorated with graffiti in homage.

Montparnasse

Hôtel Ariane €€ *35 rue de la Sablière, 75014; tel: 01 45 45 67 13; www.hotel-ariane.fr.* Peace and quiet is one of the Ariane's biggest selling points. Its 30 rooms are themed around the subject of 'time', referencing the street on which it is situated (*sablière* is hourglass in French). All have free Wi-fi and flat-screen TV.

Hôtel Istria €€ *29 rue Campagne Première, 75014; tel: 01 43 20 91 82; www.hotel-istria-paris.com.* Three star hotel, whose exotic previous guests have included Man Ray, Eric Satie and Rainer Maria Rilker. The 26 rooms are based around an attractive interior courtyard; all have flat-screen TVs and Wi-fi.

DICTIONARY

ENGLISH–FRENCH

adj adjective　**adv** adverb　**BE** British English　**n** noun　**prep** preposition　**v** verb

A

abbey l'abbaye
accept v accepter
access v accéder; n accès
accident l'accident
accommodation le logement
account le compte
acetaminophen le paracétamol
acupuncture l'acuponcture
adapter l'adaptateur
address l'adresse
admission l'entrée
after après; ~**noon** l'après-midi; ~**shave** l'après-rasage
age l'âge
agency l'agence
AIDS Déficience le Syndrome d'immunodéficience acquise
air l'air; ~ **conditioning** la climatisation; ~ **pump** la pompe à air; ~**line** la compagnie aérienne; ~**mail** par avion; ~**plane** l'avion; ~**port** l'aéroport

aisle (plane) le couloir; ~ **(theater)** l'allée; ~ **seat** le siège couloir
allergic allergique; ~ **reaction** la réaction allergique
allow v permettre
alone seul
alter v modifier
aluminum foil le papier aluminium
amazing surprenant
ambulance l'ambulance
American américain
amusement park le parc d'attractions
and et
anemic anémique
anesthesia l'anesthésie
animal l'animal
ankle la cheville
antibiotic l'antibiotique
antiques store l'antiquaire
antiseptic cream la crème antiseptique
anything rien
apartment l'appartement
appendix (body part) l'appendice

appetizer l'entrée
appointment le rendez-vous
arcade la salle de jeux
area code le code régional
arm le bras
aromatherapy l'aromathérapie
around (the corner) au coin
arrivals (airport) les arrivées
arrive v arriver
artery l'artère
arthritis l'arthrite
art l'art
Asian asiatique
aspirin l'aspirine
asthmatic asthmatique
ATM le distributeur automatique de billets; ~ **card** la carte de retrait
attack l'attaque
attend v participer
attraction (place) le lieu touristique
attractive beau
Australia l'Australie
Australian australien

automatic automatique; ~ **car** la voiture automatique
available disponible

B

baby le bébé; ~ **bottle** le biberon; ~ **wipe** la lingette pour bébé; ~**sitter** le baby-sitter
back (body part) le dos; ~**ache** le mal de dos; ~**pack** le sac à dos
bag le sac
baggage [BE] le bagage; ~ **claim** le retrait des bagages; ~ **ticket** l'étiquette
bakery la boulangerie
ballet le ballet
bandage le pansement
bank la banque
bar (place) le bar
barbecue le barbecue
barber le coiffeur pour hommes
baseball le baseball
basket (grocery store) le panier
basketball le basketball
bathroom la salle de bains

battery la pile
battleground le champ de bataille
be v être
beach la plage
beautiful beau
bed le lit; **~ and breakfast** le bed and breakfast
before avant
begin v commencer
beginner le débutant
behind derrière
beige beige
belt la ceinture
berth la couchette
best meilleur
better mieux
bicycle la bicyclette; le vélo
big grand **~ bigger** plus grand
bike route la piste cyclable
bikini le bikini; **~ wax** l'épilation à la cire du maillot
bill (charge) v facturer; ~ n **(invoice)** la facture; **~** n **(money)** la coupure; ~ n **(of sale)** le reçu
bird l'oiseau
birthday l'anniversaire
black noir
bladder la vessie
bland sans goût
blanket la couverture
bleed v saigner
blood le sang; **~ pressure** la tension

blouse le chemisier
blue bleu
board v embarquer; **~ing pass** la carte d'embarquement
boat le bateau
bone l'os
book le livre; **~store** la librairie
boots les bottes
boring ennuyant
botanical garden le jardin botanique
bother v ennuyer
bottle la bouteille; **~ opener** l'ouvre-bouteille
bowl le saladier
box la boîte
boxing match le match de boxe
boy le garçon; **~friend** le petit-ami
bra le soutien-gorge
bracelet le bracelet
brakes (car) les freins
break v **(tooth/bone)** casser
breakdown la panne
breakfast le petit déjeuner
break-in (burglary) l'effraction
breast le sein; **~feed** v allaiter
breathe v respirer
bridge pont
briefs (clothing) les slips
bring v apporter
British anglais
broken cassé

brooch la broche
broom le balai
brother le frère
brown marron
bug l'insecte
building le bâtiment
burn v brûler
bus le bus; **~ station** la gare routière; **~ stop** l'arrêt de bus; **~ ticket** le ticket de bus; **~ tour** la visite en bus
business les affaires; **~ card** la carte de visite; **~ center** le centre d'affaires; **~ class** la classe affaire; **~ hours** les heures d'ouverture
butcher le boucher
buttocks les fesses
buy v acheter
bye au revoir

C

cabaret le cabaret
cabin la cabine
cable car le téléphérique
café le café
call v appeler; **~ collect** appeler **~** n l'appel en PCV;
calories les kilocalories
camera l'appareil photo; **~ case** le sac à appareil photo; **~ store** la boutique photo
camp v camper; **~ing stove** le réchaud; **~site** le camping

can opener le l'ouvre-boîte
Canada le Canada
Canadian canadien
cancel v annuler
candy le bonbon
canned goods les conserves
canyon la gorge
car la voiture; **~ hire** **[BE]** la voiture de location; **~ park [BE]** le parking; **~ rental** la voiture de location; **~ seat** le siège bébé
carafe la carafe
card la carte; **ATM ~** la carte de retrait; **credit ~** la carte de crédit; **phone ~** le carte de téléphone
carry-on (piece of hand luggage) le bagage à main
cart le chariot
carton le paquet; **~ of cigarettes** la cartouche de cigarettes
case (amount) le cas
cash v encaisser; **~** n le liquide; **~ advance** l'avance
cashier la caisse
casino le casino
castle le château
cathedral la cathédrale
cave la grotte
CD le CD (disque compact)
cell phone le portable

Celsius Celsius

centimeter le centimètre

certificate le certificat

chair la chaise; **~ lift** le télésiège

change v (baby) changer; **~ (money)** échanger; **~** n (payment) le chèque; **~ ~** n (payment) la monnaie;

charcoal le charbon de bois

charge v (credit card) payer par carte

charge (cost) le coût

cheap bon marché

cheaper moins cher

check v (luggage) enregistrer; **~ (on something)** vérifier; **~** n (payment) le chèque; **~-in (hotel/airport)** l'enregistrement; **~ing**

account le compte courant; **~ ~-out (hotel)** quitter la chambre

Cheers! Santé!

chemical toilet les toilettes portables

chemist [BE] la pharmacie

cheque [BE] le chèque

chest (body part) la poitrine; **~ pain** la douleur à la poitrine

chewing gum le chewing-gum

child l'enfant; **~'s seat** le siège enfant

children's menu le menu enfant

children's portion la portion enfant

chopsticks les baguettes

church l'église

cigar le cigare

cigarette la cigarette

class la classe

classical music la musique classique

clean v nettoyer; **~** adj propre; **~ing product** le produit d'entretien; **~ing supplies** les produits d'entretien

clear v (on an ATM) effacer

cliff la falaise

cling film [BE] le cellophane

close v (shop) fermer; **~** adv près; **~d** fermé

clothing les vêtements; **~ store** le magasin de vêtements

club le club

coat le manteau

coffee shop le café

coin la pièce

colander la passoire

cold (sickness) le rhume; **~ (temperature)** froid

colleague le collègue

cologne l'eau de Cologne

color la couleur

comb le peigne

come v venir

complaint la plainte

computer l'ordinateur

concert le concert; **~ hall** la salle de concert

condition (medical) l'état de santé

conditioner l'après-shampooing

condom le préservatif

conference la conférence

confirm v confirmer

congestion la congestion

connect v (internet) se connecter

connection (flight) la correspondance; **~ (internet)** la connexion

constipated constipé

consulate le consulat

consultant le consultant

contact v contacter

contact lens les lentilles de contact; **~ solution** la solution pour lentilles de contact

contagious contagieux

convention hall le palais des congrès

conveyor belt le carrousel

cook v cuisiner; **~ing gas** le gaz

cool (temperature) frais

copper le cuivre

corkscrew le tire-bouchon

cost v coûter

cot le lit pliant

cotton le coton

cough v tousser; **~** n la toux

country code le code national

cover charge (bar, club) le droit d'entrée; **~ (restaurant)** le couvert

crash v (car) avoir un accident

cream (ointment) la crème

credit card la carte de crédit

crew neck le col rond

crib le berceau

crystal le cristal

cup la tasse

currency la monnaie; **~ exchange** l'échange de monnaie; **~ exchange office** le bureau de change

current account [BE] le compte courant

customs la douane

cut v couper; **~** n (injury) la coupure

cute mignon

cycling faire du vélo

D

damage v abîmer; **~d** endommagé

dance v danser; **~ club** la discothèque; **~ing** dansant

dangerous dangereux

dark sombre

date (calendar) la date

day le jour

deaf sourd

debit card la carte de retrait

deck chair la chaise longue

declare v déclarer

decline v (credit card) refuser

deeply profondément

degree (temperature) le degré

delay v retarder

delete v (computer) supprimer

delicatessen la charcuterie

delicious délicieux

denim jean

dentist le dentiste

denture le dentier

deodorant le déodorant

department store le grand magasin

departures (airport) les départs

deposit v déposer; ~ (bank) le dépôt

desert le désert

detergent le détergent

develop v (film) développer

diabetic diabétique

dial v composer

diamond le diamant

diaper la couche

diarrhea la diarrhée

diesel le gazole

difficult difficile

digital numérique; ~ **camera** l'appareil photo numérique; ~ **photo** la photo numérique

dining room la salle à manger

dinner le dîner

direction la direction

dirty sale

disabled [BE] handicapé; ~ **accessible [BE]** accessible aux handicapés

disconnect v (computer) déconnecter

discount la réduction

dish (kitchen) la vaisselle; ~**washer** le lave-vaisselle; ~**washing liquid** le détergent pour lave-vaisselle

display montrer; ~ **case** la vitrine

disposable jetable; ~ **razor** le rasoir jetable

dive v plonger; ~**ing equipment** l'équipement de plongée

divorce v divorcer

dizzy avoir des vertiges

doctor le docteur

doll la poupée

dollar (U.S.) le dollar

domestic national; ~ **flight** le vol national

door la porte

dormitory le dortoir

double bed le lit double

downtown (direction) vers le centre-ville; ~ **area** le centre-ville

dozen la douzaine

drag lift le remonte-pentes

dress (piece of clothing) la robe; ~ **code** la tenue exigée

drink v boire; ~ n la boisson; ~ **menu** la carte des boissons

drinking water l'eau potable

drive v conduire; ~**r's license** le numéro de permis de conduire

drop (medicine) la goutte

drowsiness la somnolence

dry cleaner la teinturerie

dubbed doublé

during pendant

duty (tax) la taxe

duty-free hors taxe

DVD DVD

E

ear l'oreille; ~**ache** l'otite

early tôt

earrings les boucles d'oreille

east est

easy facile

eat v manger

economy class la classe économique

elbow le coude

electric outlet la prise électrique

elevator l'ascenseur

e-mail v envoyer un mail; ~ n le mail; ~ **address** l'adresse mail

emergency l'urgence; ~ **exit** la sortie de secours

empty v vider

enamel (jewelry) l'émail

end v finir

English anglais

engrave v graver

enjoy v prendre plaisir

enter v entrer

entertainment le divertissement

entrance l'entrée

envelope l'enveloppe

equipment l'équipement

escalators l'escalator

e-ticket le billet électronique

EU resident le résident européen

euro l'euro

evening la soirée

excess l'excès

exchange v échanger; ~ n (place) le bureau de change; ~ **rate** le taux de change

excursion l'excursion

excuse v excuser

exhausted épuisé

exit v sortir; ~ n la sortie

expensive cher

expert (skill level)
l'expert
exposure (film) la
pose
express express; **~
bus** le bus direct; **~
train** l'express
extension (phone)
le poste
extra extra; ~ **large**
très grand
extract v **(tooth)**
arracher
eye l'œil
eyebrow wax
l'épilation à la cire
des sourcils

F

face le visage
facial le soin du
visage
family la famille
fan (appliance) le
ventilateur; **~ (sou-
venir)** l'éventail
far loin
farm la ferme
far-sighted presbyte
fast vite; **~ food** le
fast food
faster plus vite
fat free 0% de
matières grasses
father le père
fax v envoyer un
fax; **~** n le fax; **~
number** le numéro
de fax
feed v nourrir
ferry le ferry
fever la fièvre
field (sports) le
terrain de sport

fill v faire le plein
fill v **out (form)**
remplir
filling (tooth) le
plombage
film (camera) la
pellicule
**fine (fee for breaking
law)** la contraven-
tion
finger le doigt; **~nail**
l'ongle
fire le feu; **~ department** les pompiers;
~ door la porte
coupe-feu
first premier; **~ class**
la première classe
fitting room la cabine
d'essayage
fix v **(repair)** réparer
flashlight la lampe
torche
flat tire [tyre BE] le
pneu crevé
flight le vol
floor le sol
flower la fleur
folk music la mu-
sique folklorique
food la nourriture
foot le pied
football [BE] le
football; **~ game
[BE]** le match de
football
for pour
forecast la météo
forest la forêt
fork la fourchette
form le formulaire
formula (baby) le
lait pour bébés
fort le fort

fountain la fontaine
France la France
free libre
freezer le congélateur
French français
fresh frais
friend l'ami
frying pan la poêle
full-service le
service complet
full-time le temps
plein

G

game le match
garage le garage
garbage bag le sac
poubelle
gas l'essence; **~
station** la station
service
gate (airport) la
porte
gay gay; **~ bar** le
bar gay; **~ club** le
club gay
gel (hair) le gel
get off v **(a train,
bus, subway)**
descendre
get to v aller
gift le cadeau; **~
shop** la boutique
cadeaux
girl la fille; **~friend**
la petite-amie
give v donner
glass le verre;
glasses les lunettes
go v **(somewhere)**
aller
gold l'or
golf course le terrain
de golf

golf tournament le
tournoi de golf
good adj bon; **~** n le
produit; **~ afternoon**
bon après-midi; **~
evening** bonsoir;
~ morning bonjour;
~bye au revoir
goods les produits
gram le gramme
grandchild les
petits-enfants
grandparent les
grands-parents
gray gris
green vert
grocery store le
magasin de fruits et
légumes
ground floor le
rez-de-chaussée
groundcloth le tapis
de sol
groundsheet le drap
du dessous
group le groupe
guide le guide; **~ book**
le guide; **~ dog** le
chien d'aveugle
gym la gym
gynecologist le
gynécologue

H

hair les cheveux;
dryer le sèche-
cheveux d'étudiant;
~ salon le coiffeur;
~brush la brosse;
~cut la coupe de
cheveux; **~spray** la
laque; **~style** le
style de coiffure;
~stylist le coiffeur

half la moitié; ~
  hour la demi-heure
  ~-kilo le demi-kilo
hammer le marteau
hand la main; ~
  luggage [BE] le
  bagage à main;
  ~bag [BE] le sac
  à main
handicapped
  l'handicapé; **~-ac-**
  cessible accessible
  aux **handicapés**
hangover la gueule
  de bois
happy heureux
hat le chapeau
have v avoir
head (body part) la
  tête; **~ache** le mal
  de tête; **~phones**
  les écouteurs
health la santé;
  ~ food store le
  magasin de produits
  diététiques
heart le cœur; **~con-**
  dition le problème
  cardiaque
heat le chauffage;
  ~er le chauffage
hectare l'hectare
hello bonjour
helmet le casque
help v aider; ~ n
  l'aide
here ici
hi salut
high haut; **~chair**
  la chaise haute;
  ~-heeled shoes
  les chaussures à
  talons aiguilles;
  ~way l'autoroute

hiking boots les
  chaussures de
  marche
hill la colline
hire v [BE] louer; ~
  car [BE] la voiture
  de location
hitchhike v faire de
  l'auto-stop
hockey le hockey
holiday [BE] les
  vacances
horsetrack le champ
  de course
hospital l'hôpital
hostel l'auberge de
  jeunesse
hot (spicy) épicé;
  ~ (temperature)
  chaud; **~ spring**
  la source chaude;
  ~ water l'eau
  chaude
hotel l'hôtel
hour l'heure
house la maison;
  ~hold goods les
  produits ménagers;
  ~keeping service
  le service d'entretien
how comment; ~
  much combien
hug v enlacer
hungry faim
hurt la douleur
husband le mari

I

ibuprofen
  l'ibuprofène
ice la glace; ~
  hockey le hockey
  sur glace
icy glacé

identification
  l'identification
ill malade
in dans
include v inclure
indoor pool la piscine
  intérieure
inexpensive pas
  cher
infected infecté
information (phone)
  les renseigne-
  ments; **~ desk**
  le bureau des
  renseignements
insect l'insecte; ~
  bite la piqure
  d'insecte; ~
  repellent la lotion
  anti-insectes
insert v insérer
insomnia l'insomnie
instant message
  le message
  instantané
insulin l'insuline
insurance
  l'assurance; ~
  card la carte
  d'assurance; **~com-**
  pany la compagnie
  d'assurance
interesting intéres-
  sant
intermediate le
  niveau intermédiaire
international
  (airport area)
  l'international
  (terminal); **~ flight**
  le vol international;
  ~ student card la
  carte internationale
  d'étudiant

internet l'internet;
  ~ cafe le cyber
  café; **~ service** le
  service internet
interpreter
  l'interprète
intersection
  l'intersection
intestine l'intestin
introduce v présenter
invoice [BE] la
  facture
Ireland l'Irlande
Irish irlandais
iron v repasser; ~ n
  (clothes) le fer à
  repasser
Italian italien

J

jacket la veste
jar le pot
jaw la mâchoire
jazz le jazz; **~ club**
  le club de jazz
jeans le jean
jet ski le jet ski
jeweler la bijouterie
jewelry le bijou
join v joindre
joint (body part)
  l'articulation

K

key la clé; **~ card** la
  carte de la chambre;
  ~ ring la chaîne
kiddie pool la
  pataugeoire
kidney (body part)
  le rein
kilo le kilo; **~gram** le
  kilogramme; **~meter**
  le kilomètre

kiss v embrasser
kitchen la cuisine; ~ **foil [BE]** le papier aluminium
knee le genou
knife le couteau

L

lace la dentelle
lactose intolerant allergique au lactose
lake le lac
large grand
larger plus grand
last dernier
late (time) tard
later plus tard
laundromat la laverie automatique
laundry la lessive; ~ **facility** la buanderie; ~ **service** le service de nettoyage
lawyer l'avocat
leather le cuir
leave v partir
left (direction) à gauche
leg la jambe
lens le verre
less moins
lesson la leçon
letter la lettre
library la bibliothèque
life jacket le gilet de sauvetage
lifeguard le secouriste
lift [BE] l'ascenseur; ~ **pass** le forfait
light (cigarette)

v allumer; ~ adj **(overhead)** blond; ~**bulb** l'ampoule
lighter le briquet
like v aimer
line (train) la ligne
linen le lin
lip les lèvres
liquor store le marchand de vins et de spiritueux
liter le litre
little adv peu; ~ adj petit
live v vivre
liver (body part) le foie
loafers les mocassins
local du quartier
lock v fermer; ~ n le cadenas; ~**er** la consigne
log off (computer) terminer une session
log on (computer) ouvrir une session
long long; ~ **sleeves** les manches longues; ~~**sighted [BE]** presbyte
look v regarder
lose v **(something)** perdre
lost perdu; ~ **and found** les objets trouvés
lotion la crème
louder plus fort
love v **(someone)** aimer; ~ n amour
low bas
luggage le bagage; ~ **cart** le chariot; ~

locker la consigne; ~ **ticket** le retrait des bagages
lunch le déjeuner
lung le poumon

M

magazine le magazine
magnificent magnifique
mail le courrier; ~**box** la boîte-à-lettres
main attraction la principale attraction touristique
main course le plat principal
mall le centre commercial
man l'homme
manager le responsable
manicure la manucure
manual car la voiture manuelle
map la carte
market le marché
married marié
marry v se marier
mass (church service) la messe
massage le massage
match le match
meal le repas
measure v **(someone)** mesurer
measuring cup la mesure
measuring spoon la cuillère à doser
mechanic le mécanicien

medicine le médicament
medium (size) moyen
meet v **(someone)** rencontrer
meeting la réunion; ~ **room** la salle de réunion
membership card la carte de membre
memorial (place) le lieu commémoratif
memory card la carte mémoire **mend** v raccourcir
menstrual cramp les règles douloureuses
menu la carte
message le message
meter (parking) l'horodateur
microwave le micro-onde
midday [BE] midi
midnight minuit
mileage le kilométrage
mini-bar le mini bar
minute la minute
missing disparu
mistake l'erreur
mobile home le mobile home
mobile phone [BE] le portable
mobility la mobilité
money l'argent
month le mois
mop le serpillière
moped la mobylette
more plus
morning le matin
mosque la mosquée
mother la mère

motion sickness (air) le mal de l'air; **~ (sea)** le mal de mer

motor boat le bateau à moteur

motorcycle la mobylette

motorway [BE] l'autoroute

mountain la montagne mousse la mousse

mouth la bouche

movie le film; **~ theater** le cinéma

mug v attaquer

muscle le muscle

museum le musée

music la musique; **~ store** le disquaire

N

nail file la lime à ongle

nail salon l'onglerie

name le nom

napkin la serviette

nappies [BE] les couches

nationality la nationalité

nature preserve la réserve naturelle

nausea la nausée

near près; **~by** près de; **~-sighted** myope

neck le cou

necklace le collier

need v avoir besoin

newspaper le journal

newsstand le kiosque à journaux

next suivant

nice bien

night la nuit

nightclub le night club

no non

non-alcoholic non alcoolisé

non-smoking non fumeur

noon midi

north nord

nose le nez

note [BE] la coupure

nothing rien

notify v informer

novice (skill level) novice

now maintenant

number le nombre; le numéro

nurse l'infirmier

O

office le bureau; **~ hours** les heures d'ouverture

off-licence [BE] le marchand de vins et de spiritueux

oil l'huile

OK d'accord

old vieux

on the corner au coin

once une fois

one un; **~-way (ticket)** l'aller simple; **~-way street** le sens unique

only seulement

open v ouvrir; **~** adj ouvert

opera l'opéra; **~ house** l'opéra

opposite le contraire

optician l'opticien

orange (color) orange

orchestra l'orchestre

order v commander

outdoor pool la piscine extérieure

outside dehors

over-the-counter (medication) sans ordonnance

overlook (scenic place) le point d'observation

overnight de nuit

oxygen treatment le soin à l'oxygène

P

pacifier la tétine

pack v faire les bagages

package le colis

pad [BE] la serviette hygiénique

pain la douleur

pajamas le pyjama

palace le palais

panties les culottes

pants le pantalon

pantyhose le collant

paper le papier; **~ towel** la serviette en papier

paracetamol [BE] le paracétamol

park v se garer; **~** n le parc; **~ing garage** le garage; **~ing lot** le parking

part (for car) la pièce; **~-time** le temps partiel

pass through v passer

passenger le passager

passport le passeport; **~ control** le contrôle de passeport

password le mot de passe

pastry shop la pâtisserie

path le chemin

pay v payer; **~ phone** le téléphone public

peak (of a mountain) le sommet

pearl la perle

pedestrian le piéton

pediatrician le pédiatre

pedicure la pédicure

pen le stylo

penicillin la pénicilline

penis le pénis

per par; **~ day** par jour; **~ hour** par heure; **~ night** par nuit; **~ week** par semaine

perfume le parfum

period (menstrual) les règles; **~ (of time)** la période

permit v permettre

personal identification number (PIN) le code secret

petite menue

petrol [BE] l'essence; **~ station [BE]** la station service

pewter l'étain
pharmacy la pharmacie
phone v téléphoner; ~ n le téléphone; ~ **call** l'appel; ~ **card** la carte de téléphone; ~ **number** le numéro de téléphone
photo la photo; **~copy** la photocopie; **~graphy** la photographie
pick up v (something) prendre
picnic area l'aire de pique-nique
piece le morceau
Pill (birth control) la pilule
pillow l'oreiller
pink rose
piste [BE] la piste; ~ **map [BE]** la carte des pistes
pizzeria la pizzeria
place v (a bet) parier
plane l'avion
plastic wrap le cellophane
plate l'assiette
platform le quai
platinum platine
play v jouer; ~ n (theater) la pièce **~ground** l'aire de jeux **~pen** le parc
please s'il vous plaît
pleasure le plaisir
plunger le déboucheur de toilettes
plus size grande taille

pocket la poche
poison le poison
poles (skiing) les bâtons
police la police; ~ **report** le rapport de police; ~ **station** le commissariat de police
pond l'étang
pool la piscine
pop music la pop musique
portion la portion
post [BE] le courrier; ~ **office** le bureau de poste; **~box [BE]** la boîte-à-lettres; **~card** la carte postale
pot la casserole
pottery la poterie
pound (British sterling) la livre sterling
pregnant enceinte
prescribe v prescrire
prescription l'ordonnance
press v (clothing) repasser
price le prix
print v imprimer
problem le problème
produce v produire; ~ **store** le marchand de fruits et légumes
prohibit v interdire
pronounce v prononcer
public public
pull v (door sign) tirer

purple pourpre
purse le sac
push v (door sign) pousser
pushchair [BE] la poussette

Q

quality la qualité
question la question
quiet le silence; le calme

R

racetrack la piste de courses
racket (sports) la raquette
railway station [BE] la gare
rain la pluie; **~coat** l'imperméable; **~forest** la forêt vierge
rainy pluvieux
rap (music) le rap
rape v violer; ~ n le viol
rash l'irritation cutanée
razor blade la lame de rasoir
reach v atteindre
ready prêt
real vrai
receipt le reçu
receive v recevoir
reception la réception
recharge v recharger
recommend v recommander
recommendation la recommandation

recycling les ordures à recycler
red rouge
refrigerator le réfrigérateur
region la région
registered mail le courrier recommandé
regular ordinaire
relationship la relation
rent v louer; **~al car** la voiture de location
repair v réparer
repeat v répéter
reservation la réservation; ~ **desk** le bureau de réservation
reserve v réserver
restaurant le restaurant
restroom les toilettes
retired v prendre sa retraite
return v (something) rendre; ~ n [BE] l'aller-retour
rib (body part) la côte
right (direction) à droite; ~ **of way** le droit de passage
ring la bague
river la rivière
road map la carte routière
rob v voler
romantic romantique
room la pièce; ~ **key** la clé; ~ **service** le service de chambre

round-trip l'aller-retour
route la route
rowboat la barque
rubbish [BE] les poubelles; **~ bag [BE]** le sac poubelle
rugby le rugby
ruins les ruines

S

sad triste
safe adj en sécurité; **~** n le coffre-fort
sales tax la TVA
same le même
sandals les sandales
sanitary napkin la serviette hygiénique
saucepan la casserole
sauna le sauna
save v **(computer)** sauvegarder
savings (account) le compte épargne
scanner scanner
scarf l'écharpe
schedule v prévoir; **~** n l'horaire
science la science
scissors les ciseaux
sea la mer
seat le siège
security la sécurité
see v voir
self-service le self-service
sell v vendre
seminar le séminaire
send v envoyer
senior citizens les seniors

separated (marriage) séparés
serious sérieux
service (in a restaurant) le service
sexually transmitted disease (STD) les maladies sexuellement transmissibles
shampoo le shampooing
sharp tranchant
shaving cream la mousse à raser
sheet le drap
shirt la chemise
ship v envoyer
shoe store le magasin de chaussures
shoes les chaussures
shop v faire des achats
shopping les courses; **~ area** le quartier des magasins; **~ centre [BE]** le centre commercial; **~ mall** le centre commercial
short court; **~-sighted [BE]** myope; **~ sleeves** les manches courtes; **~s** le short
shoulder l'épaule
show v montrer
shower la douche
shrine le lieu saint
sick malade
side dish l'accompagnement
side effect l'effet secondaire

sightseeing le tourisme; **~ tour** la visite touristique
sign v signer
silk la soie
single (unmarried) adj célibataire; n **~ bed** le lit une place; **~ prints** le tirage unique; **~ room** la chambre simple
sink l'évier
sister la sœur
sit v s'asseoir
size la taille
ski v skier; **~** n le ski; **~ lift** le télésiège
skin la peau
skirt la jupe
sleep v dormir
sleeper car le wagon couchette
sleeping bag le sac de couchage
sleeping car [BE] le wagon couchette
slice la tranche
slippers les chaussons
slower plus lent
slowly lentement
small petit
smaller plus petit
smoke v fumer
smoking (area) la zone fumeur
snack bar le bar
sneakers les tennis
snorkeling equipment l'équipement de plongée
snowboard le snowboard

snowshoe la chaussure de ski
snowy neigeux
soap le savon
soccer le football; **~ game** le match de football
sock la chaussette
soother [BE] la tétine
sore throat le mal de gorge
sorry désolé
south sud
souvenir le souvenir; **~ store** le magasin de souvenirs
spa le spa
spatula la spatule
speak v parler
special (food) la spécialité; le plat typique
specialist (doctor) le spécialiste
specimen l'échantillon
speed (velocity) la vitesse
spell v épeler
spicy épicé
spine (body part) la colonne vertébrale
spoon la cuillère
sporting goods store le magasin de sport
sports le sport; **~ massage** le massage sportif
sprain l'entorse
stadium le stade
stairs les escaliers
stamp v **(a ticket)** timbrer; **~** n **(postage)** le timbre

start v **(a car)** démarrer; v **(to begin)** commencer
starter [BE] l'entrée
station la station; ~ **wagon** le break; **bus** ~ la gare routière; **gas** ~ la station service; mus‑ter ~ **[BE]** la salle d'attente; **petrol** ~ **[BE]** la station service; **subway** ~ la station de métro; **train** ~ la gare
statue la statue
stay v rester
steal v voler
steep escarpé
sterling silver l'argent fin
sting la piqûre
stolen volé
stomach l'estomac; ~**ache** les maux de ventre
stop v arrêter; ~ n l'arrêt
store directory le plan du magasin
stove la gazinière
straight droit
strange étrange
stream le ruisseau
stroller la poussette
student l'étudiant
study v étudier
stunning stupéfiant
subtitle subtil
subway le métro; ~ **station** la station de métro
suit le costume; ~**case** la valise

sun le soleil; ~ **block** l'écran solaire; ~**burn** le coup de soleil; ~**glasses** les lunettes de soleil
sunny ensoleillé
sunscreen la crème solaire
sunstroke l'insolation
super (fuel) le super; ~**market** le supermarché; ~**vision** la supervision
surfboard le surf
swallow v avaler
sweater le pull
sweatshirt le sweat-shirt
sweet (taste) sucré
sweets [BE] les bonbons
swell v gonfler
swim v nager
swimsuit le maillot de bain
symbol (keyboard) le symbole
synagogue la synagogue

T

table la table
tablet (medicine) le cachet
take v prendre
take away [BE] à emporter
tampon le tampon
taste v goûter
taxi le taxi
team l'équipe

teaspoon la cuillère à café
telephone le téléphone
temple (religious) le temple
temporary temporaire
tennis le tennis
tent la tente; ~ **peg** le piquet; ~ **pole** le pilier
terminal (airport) le terminal
terracotta la terre cuite
terrible terrible
text v **(send a message)** écrire; ~ n **(message)** le texte
thank v remercier; ~ **you** merci
that ça/cela
theater le théâtre
theft le vol
there là
thief le voleur
thigh la cuisse
thirsty soif
this ceci
throat la gorge
ticket le billet; ~ **office** la billetterie
tie (clothing) la cravate
time le temps; ~**table [BE]** les horaires
tire [tyre BE] le pneu
tired fatigué
tissues les Kleenex
to go aller

tobacconist le tabac
today aujourd'hui
toe l'orteil; ~**nail** l'ongle
toilet [BE] les toilettes; ~ **paper** le papier toilette
tomorrow demain
tongue la langue
tonight ce soir
too trop
tooth la dent; ~**paste** le dentifrice
total (amount) le total
tough (food) dur
tour la visite
tourist le touriste; ~ **information office** le syndicat d'initiative
tow truck la dépanneuse
towel la serviette
tower la tour
town la ville; ~ **hall** la mairie; ~ **map** la carte de la ville; ~ **square** le centre ville
toy le jouet; ~ **store** le magasin de jouets
track (train) le quai
traditional traditionnel
traffic light le feu tricolore
trail la piste; ~ **map** la carte des pistes
trailer la remorque
train le train; ~ **station** la gare
translate v traduire

trash les poubelles
travel *v* voyager; ~ **agency** l'agence de voyage; ~ **sickness** le mal des transports; **~er's check [cheque BE]** le chèque de voyages
tree l'arbre
trim (hair cut) *v* égaliser
trip le voyage
trolley [BE] le chariot
trousers [BE] le pantalon
T-shirt le t-shirt
turn off *v* (lights) éteindre
turn on *v* (lights) allumer
TV la télé
type *v* taper

U

ugly laid
umbrella le parapluie
unattended sans surveillance
unbranded medication [BE] le médicament générique
unconscious inconscient
underground [BE] le métro; ~ **station [BE]** la station de métro
underpants [BE] les slips
understand *v* comprendre

underwear les sous-vêtements
United Kingdom (U.K.) le Royaume Uni
United States (U.S.) les États-Unis
university l'université
unleaded (gas) sans plomb
upper supérieur
urgent urgent
use *v* utiliser
username le nom de l'utilisateur
utensil l'ustensile

V

vacancy libre
vacation les vacances
vaccination la vaccination
vacuum cleaner l'aspirateur
vagina le vagin
vaginal infection l'infection vaginale
valid valide
valley la vallée
valuable précieux
value la valeur
VAT [BE] la TVA
vegetarian végétarien
vehicle registration la carte grise
viewpoint [BE] le point d'observation
village le village
vineyard le vignoble
visit *v* visiter; **~ing hours** les heures de visite
visually impaired le malvoyant
vitamin la vitamine

V-neck le col en V
volleyball game le match de volleyball
vomit *v* vomir

W

wait *v* attendre; ~ *n* l'attente
waiter le serveur
waiting room la salle d'attente
waitress la serveuse
wake *v* réveiller; **~-up call** *n* l'appel réveil
walk *v* marcher; ~ *n* la promenade; **~ing route** le chemin de randonnée
wall clock la pendule
wallet le portefeuille
warm (something) *v* réchauffer ~ *adj* (temperature) chaud
washing machine la machine à laver
watch la montre
water skis les skis nautiques
waterfall la cascade
weather le temps
week la semaine; **~week-end** le week-end
weekly hebdomadaire
welcome *v* accueillir
well-rested bien reposé
west ouest
what quoi
wheelchair la chaise roulante; ~ **ramp** la rampe d'accès

when quand
where où
white blanc; ~ **gold** l'or blanc
who qui
widow le veuf
wife l'épouse
window la fenêtre; ~ **case** le chambranle
windsurfer le véliplanchiste
wine list la carte des vins
wireless internet l'accès Wi-Fi
wireless phone le portable
with avec
withdraw *v* retirer
withdrawal (bank) le retrait
without sans
woman la femme
wool la laine
work *v* travailler
wrap *v* emballer
wrist le poignet
write *v* écrire

Y

year l'année
yellow jaune; ~ **gold** l'or jaune
yes oui
yesterday hier
you're welcome de rien
young jeune
youth hostel l'auberge de jeunesse

Z

zoo le zoo

FRENCH-ENGLISH

A

à droite right (direction)

à gauche left (direction)

l'abbaye abbey

abîmer v damage

accéder v access

accepter v accept

l'accès Wi-Fi wireless internet

accessible aux handicapés handicapped- [disabled-BE] accessible

l'accident accident

l'accompagnement side dish

d'accord OK

accueillir v welcome

acheter v buy

l'acuponcture acupuncture

l'adaptateur adapter

l'addition bill (check)

l'adresse address; ~ **mail** e-mail address

l'aéroport airport

les affaires business

l'âge age

l'agence agency; ~ **de voyage** travel agency

l'aide n help

aider v help

aimer v like (someone); ~ v love (someone)

l'aire de jeux playground; ~ **de sport** field (sports)

l'aire de pique-nique picnic area

allaiter v breastfeed

l'allée aisle (theater)

aller v go (somewhere)

l'aller simple one-way (ticket)

allergique allergic; ~ **au lactose** lactose intolerant

l'aller-retour round-trip [return BE]

allumer v light (cigarette); ~ v turn on (lights)

l'ambulance ambulance

américain American

l'ami friend

amour n love

l'ampoule lightbulb

anémique anemic

l'anesthésie anesthesia

anglais British; English

l'animal animal

l'année year

l'anniversaire birthday

annuler v cancel

l'antibiotique antibiotic

l'antiquaire antique store

l'appareil photo camera; ~ **numérique** digital camera

l'appartement apartment

l'appel phone call

appeler v call

l'appendice appendix (body part)

apporter v bring

après after

l'après after; ~-**midi afternoon**; ~-**rasage** aftershave; ~-**shampooing** conditioner

l'arbre tree

la salle de jeux arcade

l'argent money; ~ **fin** sterling silver

l'aromathérapie aromatherapy

arracher v extract (tooth)

l'arrêt n stop; ~ **de bus** bus stop

arrêter v stop

les arrivées arrivals (airport)

arriver v arrive

l'art arts

l'artère artery

l'arthrite arthritis

l'articulation joint (body part)

l'ascenseur elevator [lift BE]

asiatique Asian

l'aspirateur vacuum cleaner

l'aspirine aspirin

l'assiette plate

l'assurance insurance

asthmatique asthmatic

l'attaque attack

attaquer v mug

atteindre v reach

attendre v wait

l'attente n wait

au coin on/around the corner

au revoir goodbye

l'auberge de jeunesse youth hostel

aujourd'hui today

l'Australie Australia

australien Australian

automatique automatic

l'autoroute highway [motorway BE]

avaler v swallow

l'avance cash advance

avant before

avec with

l'avion airplane

l'avocat lawyer

avoir v have; ~ **besoin** v need; ~ **des vertiges** dizzy; ~ **la nausée** nauseous; ~ **un accident** v crash (car)

B

le baby-sitter babysitter

le bagage à main carry-on [piece of hand luggage BE]

le bagage luggage [baggage BE]

la bague ring

les baguettes chopsticks

le balai broom

le ballet ballet

la banque bank

le bar bar (place), snack bar; **~ gay** gay bar

le barbecue barbecue

la barque rowboat

bas low

le baseball baseball

le basketball basketball

le bateau boat; **~ à moteur** motor boat

le bâtiment building

les bâtons poles (skiing)

beau attractive, beautiful

le bébé baby

le bed and breakfast bed and breakfast

beige beige

belle pretty

le berceau crib

le biberon baby bottle

la bibliothèque library

la bicyclette bicycle

bien well; **~ reposé** well-rested

le bijou jewelry

la bijouterie jeweler

le bikini bikini

la billeterie ticket office; **~ électron-ique** e-ticket

blanc white

bleu blue

boire v drink

la boisson n drink

la boîte box; **~-à-lettres** mailbox [postbox BE]

bon adj good; **~ après-midi** good afternoon; **~marché** cheap

le bonbon candy [sweet BE]

bonjour hello, good morning

bonsoir good evening

les bottes boots

la bouche mouth

le boucher butcher

les boucles d'oreille earrings

la boulangerie bakery

la bouteille bottle

la boutique photo camera store

le bracelet bracelet

le bras arm

le briquet lighter

la broche brooch

la brosse hairbrush

brûler v burn

la buanderie laundry facility

le bureau office; **~ de change** currency exchange office; **~ de poste** post office; **~ des renseignements** information desk; **~ de réservation** reservation desk

le bus bus; **~ direct** express bus

C

ça that

le cabaret cabaret

la cabine cabin; **~ d'essayage** fitting [changing BE] room

le cachet tablet (medicine)

le cadeau gift

le cadenas n lock

le café café, coffee shop

la caisse cashier

les kilocalories calories

camper v camp

le camping campsite

le Canada Canada

canadien Canadian

la carafe carafe

le carrousel conveyor belt

la carte map, card; **~ d'assurance** insurance card; **~ des boissons** drink menu; **~ de la chambre** key card; **~ de crédit** credit card; **~ d'embarquement**

boarding pass; **~ internationale d'étudiant** international student card; **~ grise** vehicle registration; **~ de membre** membership card; **~ mémoire** memory card; **~ des pistes** trail [piste BE] map; **~ postale** post-card; **~ de retrait** ATM/debit card; **~ routière** road map; **~ de téléphone** phone card; **~ de la ville** town map; **~ de visite** business card

la carte des vins wine list

la cartouche (de cigarettes) carton (of cigarettes)

le cas case (amount)

la cascade waterfall

le casino casino

le casque helmet

cassé broken

casser v break (tooth, bone)

la casserole pot, saucepan

la cathédrale cathedral

la cave cave, cellar (wine)

le CD (disque compact) CD

ce soir tonight

ceci this

la ceinture belt

cela that

célibataire single (unmarried)

le cellophane plastic wrap [cling film BE]

Celsius Celsius

le centimètre centimeter

centre center; **~ commercial** shopping mall [centre BE]; **~ d'affaires** business center; **~ ville** town square; **~-ville** downtown area

le certificat certificate

la chaîne key ring, chain

la chaise chair; **~ haute** highchair; **~ longue** deck chair; **~ roulante** wheelchair

le chambranle display window/case

la chambre simple single room

le champ field; **~ de bataille** battleground; **~ la piste de course** horsetrack

le change n exchange (place)

changer v change (baby)

le chapeau hat

le charbon de bois charcoal

la charcuterie delicatessen

le chariot cart [trolley BE]

le château castle

chaud hot, warm (temperature)

le chauffage heat (indoor)

le chauffage heater

la chaussette sock

les chaussons slippers

les chaussures shoes; **~ de ski** snowshoes; **~ à talons aiguilles** high-heeled shoes; **~ de marche** hiking boots; **~ plates** flat shoes

le chemin trail, path; **~ de randonnée** walking route

la chemise shirt

le chemisier blouse

le chèque n check [cheque BE] (payment); **~ de voyages** traveler's check [cheque BE]

cher expensive

les cheveux hair

la cheville ankle

le chewing-gum chewing gum

le chien d'aveugle guide dog

chinois Chinese

le cigare cigar

la cigarette cigarette

le cinéma movie theater

les ciseaux scissors

la classe class; **~ affaire** business class; **~ économique** economy class

la clé key

la climatisation air conditioning

le club club; **~ gay** gay club; **~ de jazz** jazz club

le code code; **~ national** country code; **~ régional** area code; **~ secret** personal identification number (PIN)

le cœur heart

le coffre-fort safe (receptacle)

le coiffeur hair salon

le coiffeur pour hommes barber

le col rond crew neck

le col en V V-neck

le colis package

le collègue colleague

le collier necklace

la colline hill

la colonne vertébrale spine (body part)

combien how much

commander v order

commencer v begin

comment how

le commissariat de police police station

la compagnie aérienne airline

la compagnie d'assurance insurance company

composer v dial

comprendre v understand

le compte account; **~ courant** checking [current BE]

account; **~ épargne** savings account

le concert concert

conduire v drive

la conférence conference

confirmer v confirm

le congélateur freezer

la congestion congestion

se connecter v connect (internet)

la connexion connection (internet, telephone)

les conserves canned goods

la consigne luggage locker

la consigne locker

constipé constipated

le consulat consulate

le consultant consultant

contacter v contact

contagieux contagious

le contraire opposite

la contravention fine (fee for breaking law)

le contrôle de passeport passport control

la correspondance change (buses); **~ connection** (flight); **~** v transfer (change trains/flights)

le costume suit

la côte rib (body part)

le coton cotton

la couche diaper [nappy BE]
la couchette berth
le coude elbow
la couleur color
le couloir aisle (plane)
le cou neck
le coup de soleil sunburn
couper v cut
la coupure bill [note BE] (money); ~ cut (injury)
le courrier mail [post BE]; ~ recommandé registered mail
court short
le coût charge (cost)
le couteau knife
coûter v cost
le couvert cover charge (restaurant)
la couverture blanket
la cravate tie (clothing)
la crème cream/lotion; ~ antiseptique antiseptic cream; ~ solaire sunscreen
le cristal crystal
la cuillère spoon; ~ à café teaspoon; ~ à doser measuring spoon
le cuir leather
la cuisine kitchen
cuisiner v cook
la cuisse thigh
le cuivre copper
les culottes panties

le cyber café internet café

D

dangereux dangerous
dans in
dansant dancing
danser v dance
la date date (calendar)
de nuit overnight
de rien you're welcome
le déboucheur de toilettes plunger
le débutant beginner
déclarer v declare
décoller v take off (plane)
déconnecter disconnect (computer)
le degré degree (temperature)
dehors outside
le déjeuner lunch
délicieux delicious
demain tomorrow
démarrer v start (an automobile)
demi half; ~-heure half hour; ~-kilo half-kilo
la dent tooth
la dentelle lace
le dentier denture
le dentifrice toothpaste
le dentiste dentist
le déodorant deodorant
la dépanneuse tow truck
les départs departures (airport)

déposer v deposit
le dépôt deposit (bank)
dernier last
derrière behind
descendre v get off (a train, bus, subway)
le désert desert
désolé sorry
le détergent detergent; ~ pour lave-vaisselle dishwashing liquid
développer v develop (film)
la déviation alternate route
diabétique diabetic
le diamant diamond
la diarrhée diarrhea
difficile difficult
dîner v dine; le ~ dinner
la direction direction
la discothèque dance club; disparu missing
disponible available
le disquaire music store
le distributeur automatique de billets automatic teller machine (ATM)
le divertissement entertainment
divorcer v divorce
le docteur doctor
le doigt finger
le dollar dollar (U.S.)
donner v give
dormir v sleep

le dortoir dormitory
le dos back (body part)
la douane customs
doublé dubbed
la douche shower
la douleur hurt, pain; ~ à la poitrine chest pain
la douzaine dozen
le drap sheet
droit straight; ~ d'entrée cover charge (bar, club)
du quartier local
DVD DVD

E

l'eau water; ~ chaude hot water; ~ de Cologne cologne; ~ potable drinking water
l'échange de monnaie currency exchange
échanger v change (money)
l'échantillon specimen
l'écharpe scarf
l'école school
les écouteurs headphones
l'écran solaire sunblock
écrire v text (send a message); ~ v write
effacer v clear (on an ATM)
l'effet secondaire side effect
l'effraction break-in (burglary)

égaliser trim (hair cut)
l'église church
l'émail enamel (jewelry)
emballer v wrap
embarquer v board
embrasser v kiss
emporter to go [take away BE] (food order)
en sécurité safe (protected)
encaisser v cash
enceinte pregnant
endommagé damaged
l'enfant child
enlacer v hug
ennuyant boring
l'enregistrement check-in (hotel, airport)
enregistrer v check (luggage)
ensoleillé sunny
l'entorse sprain
l'entrée admission; ~ appetizer [starter BE]; ~ entrance
entrer v enter
l'enveloppe envelope
envoyer v send, ship; ~ **un fax** v fax; ~ **un mail** v e-mail
l'épaule shoulder
épeler v spell
épicé hot (spicy)
l'épilation à la cire du maillot bikini wax
l'épilation à la cire des sourcils eyebrow wax

épileptique epileptic
l'épouse wife
épuisé exhausted
l'équipe team
l'équipement equipment; ~ **de plongée** diving/snorkeling equipment
l'erreur v mistake
l'escalator escalators
les escaliers stairs
escarpé steep
ennuyer v bother
l'essence gas
l'essence petrol
est east
l'esthéticienne manicurist
l'estomac stomach
et and
l'étain pewter
l'étang pond
l'état de santé condition (medical); ~ **le problème cardiaque** heart condition
les États-Unis United States (U.S.)
éteindre v turn off (lights)
l'étiquette baggage ticket
étrange strange
être v be
l'étudiant student
étudier v study
l'euro euro
l'éventail fan (souvenir)
l'évier sink
l'excès excess

l'excursion excursion
excuser v excuse
l'expert expert (skill level)
l'express express
extra extra

F

facile easy
la facture bill [invoice BE]
faim hungry
faire v make, do; ~ **des achats** v shop; ~ **de l'auto stop** v hitchhike; ~ **les bagages** v pack; ~ **les courses** shopping; ~ **le plein** v fill; se ~ **réveiller par téléphone** wake-up call; ~ **du tourisme** sightseeing; ~ **du vélo** cycling; ~ **de la vitesse** speeding
faire un virement v transfer (money)
la falaise cliff
la famille family
le fast-food fast food
fatigué tired
le fax fax
la femme woman
la fenêtre window
le fer à repasser n iron (clothes)
fermé closed
la ferme farm
fermer v close, lock
le ferry ferry
les fesses buttocks

le feu fire; ~ **tricolore** traffic light
fiancé engaged
la fièvre fever
la fille girl
le film movie
finir v end
la fleur flower
le foie liver (body part)
la fontaine fountain
le football soccer [football BE]
la forêt forest; ~ **vierge** rainforest
le forfait lift pass
le formulaire form
le fort fort
la fourchette fork
frais cool (temperature); ~ fresh
français French
la France France
les freins brakes (car)
le frère brother
froid cold (temperature)
fumer v smoke

G

le garage garage, parking garage
garer v park
le garçon boy
la gare train [railway BE] station
la gare routière bus station
gay gay
le gaz cooking gas
la gazinière stove
le gazole diesel

le gel gel (hair)
le genou knee
le gilet de sauvetage life jacket
glacé icy
la glace ice
gonfler v swell
la gorge canyon; ~ throat
goûter v taste
la goutte drop (medicine)
le gramme gram
grand large
le grand magasin department store
grande taille plus size
les grands-parents grandparent
graver v engrave
gris gray
le groupe group
la gueule de bois hangover
le guide guide, guidebook
la gym gym
le gynécologue gynecologist

H
l'handicapé handicapped [disabled BE]
haut high
hebdomadaire weekly
l'hectare hectare
l'hétérosexuel heterosexual
l'heure hour
les heures d'ouverture business/office hours

les heures de visite visiting hours
heureux happy
hier yesterday
le hockey hockey; ~ sur glace ice hockey
l'homme man
l'hôpital hospital
l'horaire schedule [timetable BE]
hors taxe duty-free
l'hôtel hotel
l'huile oil

I
l'ibuprofène ibuprofen
ici here
l'identification identification
l'imperméable raincoat
imprimer v print
inclure v include
inconscient unconscious
infecté infected
l'infection vaginale vaginal infection
l'infirmier nurse
informer v notify
l'insecte bug
insérer v insert
l'insolation sunstroke
l'insomnie insomnia
l'insuline insulin
interdire v prohibit
intéressant interesting
l'international (terminal) international (airport area)

l'internet internet; ~ sans fil wireless internet
l'interprète interpreter
l'intersection intersection
l'intestin intestine
irlandais Irish
l'Irlande Ireland
l'irritation cutanée rash
italien Italian

J
la jambe leg
le jardin botanique botanical garden
jaune yellow
le jazz jazz
le jean jeans
jean denim
jetable disposable
le jeu game
jeune young
joindre v join
jouer v play
le jouet toy
le jour day
le journal newspaper
la jupe skirt

K
le kilo kilo; ~gramme kilogram; ~métrage mileage; ~mètre kilometer; ~mètre carré square kilometer
le kiosque à journaux newsstand
les Kleenex tissue

L
le lac lake
laid ugly
la laine wool
le lait pour bébés formula (baby)
la lame de rasoir razor blade
la lampe torche flashlight
la langue tongue
la laque hairspray
la laverie automatique laundromat [launderette BE]
le lave-vaisselle dishwasher
la leçon lesson
lentement slowly
les lentilles de contact contact lens
la lessive laundry
la lettre letter
les lèvres lip
la librairie bookstore
libre free; ~ vacancy
le lieu n place; ~ commémoratif memorial (place); ~ saint shrine; ~ touristique attraction (place)
la ligne line (train)
la lime à ongle nail file
la lingette pour bébé baby wipe
le lin linen
le liquide n cash
le lit bed; ~ double double bed; ~ pliant cot
le litre liter
le livre book

la livre sterling pounds (British sterling)

le logement accommodation

loin far

long long

la lotion anti-insectes insect repellent

louer v rent (hire BE)

la lumière light (overhead)

les lunettes glasses; **~ de soleil** sunglasses

M

la machine à laver washing machine

la mâchoire jaw

le magasin store; **~ de chaussures** shoe store; **~ de jouets** toy store; **~ de produits diététiques** health food store; **~ de souvenirs** souvenir store **~ de sport** sporting goods store; **~ de vêtements** clothing store; **~ de vins et spiritueux** liquor store

le magazine magazine

magnifique magnificent

le mail e-mail

le maillot de bain swimsuit

la main hand

maintenant now

la maison house

le mal sickness; **~ de l'air** motion -sickness (air); **~ de dos** backache; **~ de gorge** sore throat; **~ de mer** motion sickness (sea); **~ de tête** headache; **~ des transports** travel sickness

malade ill, sick

les maladies sexuellement transmissibles sexually transmitted disease (STD)

malvoyant visually impaired

les manches courtes short sleeves

les manches longues long sleeves

manger v eat

le manteau coat

la manucure manicure

le marchand de fruits et légumes produce store

le marchand de vins et de spiritueux liquor store (off-licence BE)

le marché market

marcher v walk

le mari husband

marié married

la mairie town hall

se marier v marry

marron brown

le marteau hammer

le massage massage

le match n match; **~ de boxe** boxing match; **~ de football** soccer (football BE) game; **~ de volleyball** volleyball game

le matin morning

le maux de ventre stomachache

le mécanicien mechanic

le médicament medicine

meilleur best

le même same

le menu menu; **~ enfant** children's menu

la mer sea

merci thank you

la mère mother

le message message; **~ instantané** instant message

la messe mass (church service)

la mesure measuring cup

mesurer to measure (someone)

la météo forecast

le mètre carré square meter

le métro subway (underground BE)

le micro-onde microwave

midi noon (midday BE)

mieux better

mignon cute

le mini bar mini-bar

minuit midnight

la minute minute

le mobile home mobile home

la mobilité mobility

la mobylette moped

les mocassins loafers

modifier v alter

moins less; **~ cher** cheaper

le mois month

la moitié half

la monnaie n change (money); **~ currency**

la montagne mountain

la montre watch

montrer v show

le morceau piece

la mosquée mosque

le mot de passe password

la moto motorcycle

la mousse mousse; **~ à raser** shaving cream

moyen medium (size)

le muscle muscle

le musée museum

la musique music; **~ classique** classical music; **~ folklorique** folk music

myope near- (short-BE) sighted

N

nager v swim

national domestic

la nationalité nationality

neigeux snowy

nettoyer v clean
le nez nose
le night club nightclub
le niveau intermédiaire intermediate
noir black
le nom name; ~ **de l'utilisateur** username
non no; ~ **alcoolisé** non-alcoholic; ~ **fumeur** non-smoking
nord north
nourrir v feed
le novice novice (skill level)
de nuit overnight
la nuit night
numérique digital
le numéro number; ~ **de fax** fax number; ~ **de permis de conduire** driver's license -number; ~ **de téléphone** phone number

O
les objets trouvés lost and found
l'œil eye
l'oiseau bird
l'ongle fingernail, toenail
l'opéra opera
l'opticien optician
l'or gold; ~ **blanc** white gold; ~ **jaune** yellow gold
orange orange (color)
l'orchestre orchestra
ordinaire regular

l'ordinateur computer
l'ordonnance prescription
les ordures à recycler recycling
l'oreille ear
l'oreiller pillow
l'orteil toe
l'os bone
l'otite earache
où where
ouest west
oui yes
ouvert open
l'ouvre-bouteille/boîte bottle/can opener
ouvrir v open; ~ **une session** v log on (computer)

P
le palais palace
le palais des congrès convention hall
le panier basket (grocery store)
la panne breakdown
le pansement bandage
le pantalon pants [trousers BE]
le papier paper; ~ **aluminium** aluminum [kitchen BE] foil; ~ **toilette** toilet paper
le paquet carton
par by; ~ **avion** airmail; ~ **heure** per hour; ~ **jour** per day; ~ **nuit** per night; ~ **semaine** per week

le paracétamol acetaminophen [paracetamol BE]
le parapluie umbrella
le parc playpen; ~ **park; ~ d'attractions** amusement park
le parfum perfume
parier to place (a bet)
le parking parking lot [car park BE]
parler v speak
participer v attend
pas cher inexpensive
le passager passenger
le passeport passport
passer v pass through
la passoire colander
la pataugeoire kiddie pool
la pâtisserie pastry shop
payer v pay; ~ **par carte** v charge (credit card)
la peau skin
le pédiatre pediatrician
la pédicure pedicure
le peigne comb
la pellicule film (camera)
pendant during
la pendule wall clock
la pénicilline penicillin
le pénis penis
perdre v lose (something)
perdu lost
le père father

la période period (of time)
la perle pearl
permettre v allow
la perte discharge (bodily fluid)
petit small
le petit child, small; **--ami** boyfriend; **--amie** girlfriend; ~ **déjeuner** breakfast
les petits-enfants grandchildren
peu little
la pharmacie pharmacy [chemist BE]
la photo photo; **~copie** photocopy; **~graphie** photography; ~ **numérique** digital photo
la pièce coin; ~ part (for car); ~ n play (theater); ~ room
le pied foot
le piéton pedestrian
la pile battery
le pilier tent pole
la pilule Pill (birth control)
le piquet tent peg
la piqûre sting; ~ **d'insecte** insect bite
la piscine pool; ~ **intérieure** indoor pool; ~ **extérieure** outdoor pool
la piste trail [piste BE]; ~ **cyclable** bike route
la pizzeria pizzeria
la plage beach

la plainte complaint
le plaisir pleasure
le plan du magasin store directory
le plat principal main course
platine platinum
le plombage filling (tooth)
plonger v dive
la pluie rain
plus more; ~ **bas** lower; ~ **fort** louder; ~ **grand** larger; ~ **lent** slower; ~ **petit** smaller; ~ **tard** later; ~ **tôt** earlier; ~ **vite** faster
pluvieux rainy
le pneu tire [tyre BE]; ~ **crevé** flat tire [tyre BE]
la poche pocket
la poêle frying pan
le poignet wrist
le point d'observation overlook [viewpoint BE] (scenic place)
le poison poison
la poitrine chest (body part)
la police police
la pompe à air air pump
les pompiers fire department
le pont bridge
la pop musique pop music
le portable wireless/ cell [mobile BE] phone

la porte gate (airport); ~ door; ~ **coupe-feu** fire door
le portefeuille wallet
la portion portion; ~ **enfant** children's portion
la pose exposure (film)
le poste extension (phone)
le pot jar
la poterie pottery
la poubelle garbage [rubbish BE]
le poumon lung
la poupée doll
pour for
pourpre purple
pousser to push (door sign)
la poussette stroller [pushchair BE]
précieux valuable
premier first
la première classe first class
prendre v pick up (something); ~ v take; ~ **plaisir** v enjoy; ~ **sa retraite** retired
près close, near; ~ **de** nearby
presbyte far- [long- BE] sighted
prescrire to prescribe
présenter v introduce
le préservatif condom
prévoir v schedule
la principale attraction

touristique main attraction
la prise électrique electric outlet
le prix price
le problème problem
produire produce
le produit product; ~ **d'entretien** cleaning product; ~ **ménager** household good
profondément deeply
la promenade walk
prononcer v pronounce
propre clean
public public
le pull sweater
le pyjama pajamas

Q

le quai n track [platform BE] (train)
la qualité quality
quand when
le quartier des magasins shopping area
la question question
qui who
quitter la chambre check-out (hotel)
quoi what

R

raccourcir v to shorten
la rampe d'accès wheelchair ramp
le rap rap (music)
le rapport de police police report
la raquette racket (sports)

le rasoir jetable disposable razor
la réaction allergique allergic reaction
la réception reception
recevoir v receive
recharger v recharge
le réchaud camping stove
réchauffer v warm (something)
recommandation recommendation
recommander v recommend
le reçu n bill, receipt (of sale)
recycler recycling
la réduction discount
le réfrigérateur refrigerator
refuser v decline (credit card)
regarder v look
la région region
les règles period (menstrual)
les règles douloureuses menstrual cramps
le rein kidney (body part)
la relation relationship
remercier v thank
le remonte-pentes drag lift
la remorque trailer
remplir v fill out (form)
rencontrer v meet (someone)

le rendez-vous appointment

rendre v return (something)

les renseignements information (phone)

réparer v fix (repair)

le repas meal

repasser v iron

répéter v repeat

la réservation reservation

la réserve naturelle nature preserve

réserver v reserve

le résident européen EU resident

respirer v breathe

le responsable manager

le restaurant restaurant

rester v stay

retarder v delay

retirer v withdraw

le retrait withdrawal (bank); ~ des bagages baggage claim

la réunion meeting

réveiller v wake

le rez-de-chaussée ground floor

le rhume cold (sickness)

rien anything, nothing

la rivière river

la robe dress (piece of clothing)

romantique romantic

rose pink

rouge red

la route route

le Royaume Uni United Kingdom (U.K.)

le rugby rugby

les ruines ruins

le ruisseau stream

S

s'asseoir v sit

s'il vous plaît please

le sac bag, purse; ~à dos backpack; ~ à appareil photo camera case; ~ couchage sleeping bag; ~ à main purse [handbag BE]; ~ poubelle garbage [rubbish BE] bag

le sachet bag

saigner v bleed

le saladier bowl

sale dirty

la salle room: ~ d'attente waiting room; ~ de concert concert hall; ~ à manger dining room; ~ de réunion meeting room

le salon d'essayage fitting room

salut hi

les sandales sandals

le sang blood

sans without; ~ 0% de matières grasses fat free; ~ ordonnance over the counter (medication); ~ plomb unleaded (gasoline); ~ surveillance unattended

la santé health

Santé! Cheers!

le sauna sauna

sauvegarder v save (computer)

le savon soap

le scanner scanner

la science science

le sèche-cheveux hair dryer

le secouriste lifeguard

la sécurité security

le sein breast

le self-service self-service

la semaine week

le séminaire seminar

les seniors senior citizens

le sens unique one-way street

séparé separated (marriage)

sérieux serious

la serpillière mop; ~ groundcloth

le serveur waiter

la serveuse waitress

le service service (in a restaurant); ~ de chambre room service; ~ complet full-service; ~ d'entretien housekeeping services; ~ internet internet service; ~ de nettoyage laundry service

la serviette napkin, towel; ~ hygiénique sanitary napkin [pad BE]

seul alone

seulement only

le shampooing shampoo

le short shorts

le siège seat; ~ bébé car seat; ~ couloir aisle seat; ~ enfant child's seat

signer v sign

le silence quiet

le ski ski; ~ jet jet ski

skier v ski

les skis nautiques water skis

les slips briefs [underpants BE] (clothing)

le snowboard snowboard

la sœur sister

la soie silk

soif thirsty

le soin à l'oxygène oxygen treatment

le soin du visage facial

la soirée evening

le sol floor

le soleil sun

la solution pour lentilles de contact contact lens solution

sombre dark

le sommet peak

la somnolence drowsiness

la serviette en papier paper towel

la sortie exit; ~ de secours emergency exit

sortir to exit
la source chaude hot spring
sourd deaf
les sous-vêtements underwear
le soutien-gorge bra
le souvenir souvenir
le spa spa
la spatule spatula
le spécialiste specialist (doctor)
le sport sports
le stade stadium
la station station; **~ de métro** subway [underground BE] station; **~ service** gas [petrol BE] station
la statue statue
stupéfiant stunning
le style de coiffure hairstyle
le stylo pen
subtil subtitle
sucré sweet (taste)
sud south
suivant next
le super super (fuel)
supérieur upper
le supermarché supermarket
la supervision supervision
supprimer v delete (computer)
le surf surfboard
surprenant amazing
le sweat-shirt sweatshirt
le symbole symbol (keyboard)

la synagogue synagogue
le syndicat d'initiative tourist information office
le Syndrome d'immuno-déficience acquise (SIDA) AIDS

T

le tabac tobacconist
la table table
la taille size
le tampon tampon
frapper v (computer) type
le tapis de sol groundcloth
tard late (time)
la tasse cup
le taux de change exchange rate
la taxe duty (tax)
le taxi taxi
la teinturerie dry cleaner
la télé TV; **~le téléphérique** cable car; **~le téléphone** phone; **~le téléphone public** pay phone
téléphoner v phone
le télésiège chair lift
le temple temple (religious)
temporaire temporary
le temps time, weather; **~ partiel** part-time; **~ plein** full-time
le tennis tennis

les tennis sneakers
la tension blood pressure
la tente tent
la tenue exigée dress code
le terminal terminal (airport)
terminer une session v log off (computer)
le terrain field, course; **~ de golf** golf course
la terre cuite terracotta
terrible terrible
la tête head (body part)
la tétine pacifier [soother BE]
le texte text (message)
le théâtre theater
le ticket ticket; **~ de bus** bus ticket
le timbre stamp (postage)
le tirage unique single prints
le tire-bouchon corkscrew
tirer v pull (door sign)
les toilettes restroom [toilet BE]
les toilettes portables chemical toilet
tôt early
total total (amount)
la tour tower
le touriste tourist
le tournoi de golf golf tournament
tousser v cough

tout de suite right of way
la toux cough
traditionnel traditional
traduire v translate
le train train
tranchant sharp
la tranche slice
travailler v work
très grand extra large
triste sad
trop too
le t-shirt T-shirt
la TVA sales tax [VAT BE]

U

un one
une fois once
l'université university
l'urgence emergency
urgent urgent
l'ustensile utensil
les produits d'entretien cleaning supplies
utiliser v use

V

les vacances vacation [holiday BE]
la vaccination vaccination
le vagin vagina
la vaisselle dish (kitchen)
la valeur value
valide valid
la valise suitcase
la vallée valley

végétarien vegetarian

le véliplanchiste windsurfer

le vélo tout terrain (VTT) mountain bike

vendre v sell

venir v come

le ventilateur fan (appliance)

vérifier v check (on something)

le verre glass, lens

vert green

la vessie bladder

la veste jacket

les vêtements clothing

le veuf widowed

vider v empty

vieux old

le vignoble vineyard

le village village

la ville town

le viol rape

violer v rape

le visage face

la visite tour; **~ en bus** bus tour

la visite touristique sightseeing tour

visiter v visit

la vitamine vitamin

vite fast

la vitrine display case

vivre v live

voir v see

la voiture car; **~ automatique** automatic car; **~ de location** car rental [hire BE]; **~ de location** rental [hire BE] car; **~ manuelle** manual car

le vol flight; **~ theft; ~ national** domestic flight; **~ international** international flight

volé stolen

voler v rob, steal

le voleur thief

vomir v vomit

le voyage trip

vrai real

W

le wagon couchette sleeper [sleeping BE] car

le week-end weekend

wireless internet wireless internet service

Z

la zone fumeur smoking (area)

le zoo zoo

INDEX

Berlitz pocket guide

PARIS

Twentieth Edition 2019

Editor: Zara Sekhavati
Authors: Martin Gostelow, Simon Cropper and Tatiana Wilde
Head of DTP and Pre-Press: Rebeka Davies
Managing Editor: Carine Tracanelli
Picture Editor: Tom Smyth
Cartography Update: Carte
Photography Credits: AKG 21; Alamy 52, 99; Dreamstime 87; Getty 15; Ilpo Musto/ Apa Publications 5M, 26, 55, 75, 97; iStock 1, 4ML, 4TL, 5T, 6L, 17, 18, 29, 35, 40, 45, 46, 50, 59, 65, 72, 81, 89; Kevin Cummins/Apa Publications 5MC, 6R, 11, 38, 42, 61, 66, 69, 70, 83; Ming Tang-Evans/Apa Publications 4TC, 4MC, 5TC, 5MC, 5M, 7, 7R, 13, 33, 37, 49, 62, 73, 77, 79, 85, 90, 93, 94, 101, 102, 105, 106; Shutterstock 30, 51, 57; Sylvaine Poitau/Apa Publications 23
Cover Picture: iStock

Distribution
UK, Ireland and Europe: Apa Publications (UK) Ltd; sales@insightguides.com
United States and Canada: Ingram Publisher Services; ips@ingramcontent.com
Australia and New Zealand: Woodslane; info@woodslane.com.au
Southeast Asia: Apa Publications (SN) Pte; singaporeoffice@insightguides.com
Worldwide: Apa Publications (UK) Ltd; sales@insightguides.com

Special Sales, Content Licensing and CoPublishing
Insight Guides can be purchased in bulk quantities at discounted prices. We can create special editions, personalised jackets and corporate imprints tailored to your needs. sales@insightguides.com; www.insightguides.biz

Contact us
Every effort has been made to provide accurate information in this publication, but changes are inevitable. The publisher cannot be responsible for any resulting loss, inconvenience or injury. We would appreciate it if readers would call our attention to any errors or outdated information. We also welcome your suggestions; please contact us at: berlitz@apaguide.co.uk www.insightguides.com/berlitz